CUSTOMARY LAW IN PRACTICE

CUSTOMARY LAW IN PRACTICE

by

J. G. STORRY J.P., Advocate

of Gray's Inn, Barrister

Author of *Rhodesian Criminal Practice*

JUTA & COMPANY LIMITED

CAPE TOWN WETTON JOHANNESBURG

First Published 1979

P.O. Box 123, Kenwyn 7790

ISBN 0 7021 1013 2

PRINTED AND BOUND IN THE REPUBLIC OF SOUTH AFRICA BY
THE RUSTICA PRESS (PTY.) LTD., WYNBERG, CAPE

780

PREFACE

Over the years there have been several authoritative works devoted to customary law in Rhodesia. In particular, Dr Holleman's *Shona Customary Law*, essentially a thesis for the degree of Doctor of Philosophy, sought to explain the workings of customary law within tribal society. More recently, in the Hon Mr Justice Goldin and Dr Gelfand's *African Law and Custom in Rhodesia* there are more definitive assessments of the substantive law, both as it has evolved and within the sociological context.

Paradoxically, the practice of customary law in tribal society has certain similarities with the original establishment of Equity, and decisions may still, from time to time, follow the inclination of the moment, in the name of conscience. Indeed, courts are enjoined specifically - 'in cases where no express rule is applicable to any controversy' to 'apply the principles of justice, equity and good conscience' - *vide* 3(4) of the African Law and Tribal Courts Act *(Chapter 237)*. But, inevitably, there has been a tendency among lawyers whose training devolves from the practice of a different system of law, to favour the construction of a body of precedent and to apply the same principles to similar facts. So that few lawyers, in seeking to apply or interpret customary law in a developing society are likely to quarrel with Lord Nottingham's dictum that 'with such a conscience as is only *naturalis et interna*, this court has nothing to do; the conscience by which I am to proceed is merely *civilis et politica*, and tied to certain measures; it is infinitely better for the public that a trust, security, or agreement, which is wholly secret, should miscarry, than that men should lose their estates by the mere fancy and imagination of a chancellor' - *Cook* v *Fountain* (1676) 3 Swans 585.

As the century has progressed, so greater attention has been paid to the needs of customary law and the desire to do justice between those persons whose daily lives are still largely governed by a social order to which the common law is alien. In the course of this development a body of precedent has been established, and a common code of practice endeavours to ensure the administration of justice equitably. It is with these aspects of customary law, rather than with the substantive law, that this book is concerned.

Understandably, because it would have changed the character and aim of his research, Dr Holleman refrained from consulting the decisions of the High Court and the Court of Appeal for African Civil Cases. For the purpose of seeking to understand the manner in which customary law is practised, however, reference to such decisions is essential, for they set precedent and indicate the development of the law. As was noted in *Everest Dube* v *Chief Myinga* 1965 AAC 1, customary law is not static, and is as subject to change as the common law.

That said, it is as well to point out that I have been concerned to restrict the contents of this handbook to attempt an elucidation of customary law practice, as manifested by judicial interpretation and the application of the relevant statutes. If justification for this policy is sought, then it may be found, I think, in the number of Practice Notes which the Court of Appeal has found it necessary to issue year by year - as many as eleven in one recent volume of the Reports and Decisions of the Court of Appeal for African Civil Cases. My aim has been, therefore, to cater primarily for the requirements of practitioners and, with deference, those judicial officers whose duties bring them into contact with customary law. Consequently, although a glossary of the more common customary law terms has been included for convenience, there is no exposition of substantive law, for which recourse should be had to the works listed in the bibliography.

Two further points require notice. Firstly, the

term 'common law' (by which is meant Roman-Dutch Law as modified by the statute law of Rhodesia) is used throughout solely to distinguish it from 'customary law'. Secondly, since customary law takes a fairly pragmatic view of seduction, treating the girl's father as the injured party and thus the proper person to receive compensation, on the ground that her value on the marriage mart is diminished and his financial prospects adversely affected thereby - *Kapasi* v *Magwayi* 1937 SRN 10 - and permits of no action for the recovery of damages by the girl herself - *Nira* v *Marete and Ngando* 1947 SRN 175 - this subject is dealt with in the chapter on Family Law rather than that concerned with Delict. For more obvious, though not dissimilar reasons, adultery is also included in the same chapter, rather than elsewhere.

Finally, I wish to express my thanks to His Honour Judge F C Blackie, for his encouragement and assistance in the course of preparation of the manuscript, and also for his interest, as President of the Court of Appeal for African Civil Cases, in the actual publication thereof.

J G STORRY

Vintcent Building,
Salisbury

4 December 1978

CONTENTS

PREFACE iii

BIBLIOGRAPHY AND ABBREVIATIONS ix

TABLE OF CASES xi

Chapter 1: General Principles of Application and Jurisdiction 1

A: Ascertainment and Application .. 1

B: Jurisdiction of Courts .. 5

Chapter II: Procedure and Evidence 12

A: Procedure in District Commissioners' Courts .. 12

Section 1: *Commencement of Proceedings* .. 13

Section 2: *Conduct of Proceedings* 15

Section 3: *Judgment and Appeal* .. 24

B: Procedure in the Court of Appeal 29

C. Evidence 35

Chapter III: Family Law 42

A: Marriage and Divorce .. 42

Section 1: *Lobolo* 42

Section 2: *Civil Marriage* .. 50

Section 3: *Customary Marriage* .. 52

B: Women 58

C: Children 63

Chapter III (*contd.*)

Section 1: *Children of a Christian Marriage* 63

Section 2: *Children of a Customary Marriage* 65

Section 3: *Illegitimate Children* .. 70

Chapter IV: Delict, Real and Personal Rights .. 74

A: Delict 74

B: Real Rights 79

Section 1: *Ownership* .. 79

Section 2: *Succession* .. 80

Section 3: *Personal Rights* .. 83

Appendix I : District Commissioners' Court Rules 85

Appendix II: Rules of the Court of Appeal for African Civil Cases .. 124

GLOSSARY OF CUSTOMARY LAW TERMS .. 129

INDEX 133

BIBLIOGRAPHY

Bullock, C, *The Mashona and the Matabele*, Juta & Co, Cape Town (1950).

Child, H, *The History and Extent of Recognition of Tribal Law in Rhodesia*, Min. of Internal Affairs, Salisbury (1965).

Goldin, the Hon Mr Justice, & Gelfand, Dr M, *African Law and Custom in Rhodesia*, Juta & Co, Cape Town (1975).

Holleman, J F, *Shona Customary Law*, Manchester University Press, London (1952).

Leslie, R D, *The Recognition of Tribal Law in Southern Rhodesia* (unpublished - thesis for the degree of Master of Laws of the University of Cape Town - 1963).

ABBREVIATIONS

SR	-	Southern Rhodesia Reports (1911 - 1955).
SRN/CAR	-	Reports and Decisions of the Court of Appeal for Native Civil Cases (1928-1963).
AAC	-	Reports and Decisions of the Court of Appeal for African Civil Cases (1964-date).
R&N	-	Rhodesia and Nyasaland Reports (1956-1964).
RLR	-	Rhodesian Law Reports (1964 - date).

TABLE OF CASES

A.

	Page
Aaron Jaravasi *v* Tembekire 1959 SRN 662	35
Aaron *v* Mbosha 1938 SRN 19	33
Abigail Chiutsu *v* Dennies Garisa 1969 AAC 70 ..	51
Adinisi *v* George 1969 AAC 36	71
Aggrey Chingombe *v* Tonderi Mudzi 1973 AAC 32 ..	60
Alick *v* Solomon 1967 AAC (viii)	13
Ally Musaka *v* Elizabeth Matope 1959 SRN 622 ..	68
Amon *v* Marika & Chikanda 1954 SRN 422	44
Amon Nyakunhuwa *v* Elizabeth Hove 1970 AAC 36 ..	43
Amon Nyamupfukudza *v* Dorothy a/b Chiekeni 1968 AAC 1	75
Anafi Robert *v* Annie Isiah 1964 AAC 55	64
Andrea *v* Mangarayi 1966 AAC 32	76
Angeline Chiutsu *v* Dennies Garisa 1969 AAC 70	51
Antony Muchabaiwa Marimo *v* Adelheid Marimo 1976 AAC 26	68
Arinesi & Shawati Nguwa *v* Elias 1964 AAC 63 ..	65
Augustine *v* Godwin 1976 AAC (ii)	36, 61
Augustine Mupfuni *v* Aaron Jacha 1973 AAC (v) ..	36

B.

Bachi Vela *v* M'Bayiwa Jack 1953 SRN 361	68
Baliwe Rabson *v* Nasu Obert 1972 AAC 25	25
Beatrice & Njambwa *v* James 1944 SRN 46	51
Bebura *Ex p.* 1959 SRN 627	31
Ben Mhandu Tsodzo *v* Simon Chideme 1977 AAC 22 ..	35
Ben *v* Juhana & Jowaki Antonio 1958 SRN 523 ..	65
Benjamin Mackenzie *v* Chambulangauda 1971 AAC (v)	65
Bessie *v* Ruwashe 1970 AAC 48	67
Bezai *v* Tamisayi 1969 AAC 58	81
Bowen Sibanda *v* Aidah Mpofu & Jacob Hanyana 1964 AAC 44	54
Bulawayo *v* Muchenje 1976 AAC 18	61

C.

Chada *v* Paurai 1948 SRN 189	47
Chadawa *v* Goro 1959 (1) R&N 188 (NACSR)	5
Chakara *v* Goro 1959 SRN 644	75

Page

Chamunorgwa *v* Dzokera & Sungayi 1946 SRN 101 .. 48
Chamunorgwa *v* Nyamayaro Timothy 1958 SRN 602 .. 62
Chamurwa *v* Elizabeth Chakava 1947 SRN 153 .. 59
Chanakira *v* Daka 1966 AAC 20 .. .. 27, 34
Chanakira *v* Sande 1951 SRN 268 20
Changara *v* Office 1966 AAC 18 25
Chapotoka *v* Mugombi 1941 SRN 134 48
Chari *v* Mathew 1970 AAC (vi) 19, 21
Charles Ndhlovu *v* Mketwa Ndhlovu 1971 AAC 37 .. 72
Charumbira *v* Mariye Makanda 1977 AAC 20 .. 28
Chawa *v* Bvuta 1928 SR 28 55
Chichetu *v* Mrs A Chichetu 1977 AAC 27 76
Chidombgwe *v* Nyadakudga 1949 SRN 223 71
Chiduku *v* Samiyele 1944 SRN 23 17
Chief Namauzwe *v* Shumba 1975 AAC (v) 18
Chigwida *v* Mazengera 1962 SRN (vi) 21
Chikaisa *v* Amos 1962 SRN 15 58
Chikandiwa *v* Kraalhead Masiya 1973 AAC 11 .. 6
Chikanya *v* Chigwada 1929 SRN 21 49
Chikosi *v* Chikosi(2) 1973 (1) RLR 199 (GD) .. 69
Chikuwanyanga *v* Mupariwa 1969 AAC 83 24
Chimbi *v* Chitumba 1975 AAC (v) 18
Chinyai *v* Norris 1963 CAR (vii) 35
Chinywerwe *v* Jessina 1953 SRN 333 51
Chipazura *v* Tigere 1941 SRN 130 .. 39, 43
Chiramba *v* Elinah 1964 AAC 67 30
Chirimanyemba *v* Msau 1928 SRN 1 45
Chitaguta *v* Esta & Masivambiri 1944 SRN 31 .. 47
Chokumarara, R *v*. 1945 SR 88 52
Chote *v* Matiye 1974 (1) RLR 302 (AD) .. 43, 44
Chris Faranando *v* Loido Karasa Nyuru 1976 AAC 66 61
Christopher Bzwifu *v* Chipo a/b Mica Zisengwe 1969 AAC (xi) 55
Clarkson Nkomo *v* Jonathan Jabangwe 1965 AAC (viii) 25
Cook *v* Fountain (1676) 3 Swans 585 iv
Cosmos *v* Makoni 1970 AAC 18 32
Crispen Makugutu *v* Peter Sibanda 1966 AAC 15 .. 15
Cyprian Hamandishe *v* Soda Mupambari 1968 AAC 16 78
Cyril Mangwende *v* Frank Mbanje 1961 SRN 936 .. 14

D.

Dabiya *v* Tichareva 1963 CAR (viii) 24

Page

Daniel *v* Agness Tinarwo 1966 AAC 39 78
Daniel Mbaira *v* Britto Maswi 1970 AAC (xi) .. 31
Daniel *v* Teresa 1972 AAC 17 45
David Milase *v* Witness 1958 SRN 486 69
David Moyo a/b Baita *v* Richard 1953 SRN 327 .. 16
David *v* Phillimon 1967 AAC 1 56
Davius *v* Tigere 1967 AAC (viii) 6
Dayimano *v* Kgaribaitse 1931 SR 134 .. 44, 50, 63
Denere *v* Andinowangu 1934 SRN 62 25
Dennis *v* Mhlungwa 1952 SRN 309 28
De Souza *v* Munjoma 1951 SRN 260 72
Dodo *v* Makawaya 1934 SRN 75 45
Dokotera *v* The Master of the High Court 1957 R&N 697 (SR) 83
Dolika & Kalamizu *v* Musadene 1954 SRN 420 .. 54
Dominic & anor *v* John Mujongonda 1970 AAC 6 .. 75
Dudzai *v* Mapanda 1943 SRN 20 48
Duma *v* Madidi 1918 SR 59 .. .. .. 4, 81
Dumase & Sailos Chekani *v* Adamu 1958 SRN 594 52, 66
Dune *v* Nyamuru 1945 SRN 66 56
Dzingirai Murefu *v* Rombesai Musori 1971 AAC (v) 19

E.

Edward Jelasi *v* Irene 1971 AAC 3 84
Edward Ndhlovu *v* Dogo Malaba 1959 SRN 639 .. 60
Edwin Momeshore *v* Kennie Chirume 1971 AAC 30 76
Elias Machida *v* Philemon 1964 AAC 29 83
Elias Murove *v* Edward Bernard Chakaizira 1975 AAC 33 49
Elina *v* Julius 1963 CAR (ix) 22
Elinah Ndebele & Fani Ndebele *v* Piton Ncube 1965 AAC 44 77
Elisa & Musonda *v* Lavu 1949 SRN 228 .. .. 16, 68
Elizabeth *v* Enella a/b John Zachasy 1966 AAC (xiv) 16
Elizabeth Makola *v* Gondongwe 1954 SRN 407 .. 15, 58
Elizabeth & Mzele *v* Gwandibva 1941 SRN 121 .. 72
Ellen *v* Jim 1931 SR 118 50
Elliot Mhlanga *v* Grace Weston Mundicha 1970 AAC 33 43
Elliot Ncube *v* Pesuliana Phiri 1969 AAC 9 .. 31
Emily Nkono *v* Esther Nkala 1967 AAC (vii) .. 34

Page

Eneas Hove *v* Marara 1973 AAC 34 60
Enita Marechera a/b Jeremiah Marechera *v* Naome Chidziva a/b Chamundorwa Martin Chidziva 1969 AAC (ix) 13
Enock Godfrey *v* Nediyo 1961 SRN 21 .. 32
Enock Kumalo *v* Themra Dumeya Nkomo 1973 AAC (viii) 19
Enock *v* Davide 1959 SRN 657 57
Erikanos Mupasiri *v* Maggie a/b Mufandaedza 1968 AAC 5 53
Esnad Ndebele & Josiah *v* Togo Ndebele 1965 AAC 23 64
Etrudi & Mutadzi *v* Chimondo 1960 SRM 671 .. 38
Everest Dube *v* Chief Myinga 1965 AAC 1 .. iv, 2, 61
Eveline Gumbo *v* Langton Muyambo 1969 AAC (v).. 55

F.

Fani Sibanda *v* Elijah 1956 SRN 507 60
Fanwell Chamboko *v* Jonasi Nyamayovo 1972 AAC 1 .. 84
Fanyana *v* Nyika Magwisi 1969 AAC 63 35
Fibion Zinyemba *v* Freddy Baya 1966 AAC 40 .. 57
Flora Sebetso *v* Maxwell Sebetso Rathuso 1946 SRN 119 .. .. 50, 52
Fordson Manduna *v* Clara Khanye 1977 AAC 9 .. 70
Francisca a/b Simon *v* Matope 1953 SRN 250 .. 67
Francisco *v* Sikupa 1940 SRN 82 80
Freddie Mavunga *v* Anna Murape 1970 AAC 27 .. 55
Funnwell *v* Simon 1970 AAC 25 75

G.

Gabriel Tayengwa *v* Tuburayi 1976 AAC 11 .. 60
Gahadzikwa *v* Ednah 1965 AAC (viii) 55
Gamanya *v* Saida Kakora 1958 SRN 587 .. .. 37, 62
Ganda *v* Chinamo 1946 SRN 110 63
Garadi *v* Annah 1959 SRN 663 63
Gariwa *v* Chigwedere Musarurgwa 1958 SRN 533 .. 49
Gatsi *v* Dokari 1932 SRN 51 .. .. .. 17, 64
Gatsi Kasukwere *v* Josaiah Danarembgwa 1961 SRN 7 77
George *v* Garaza 1948 SRN 187 74
George Maswimbo *v* Stanley 1965 AAC 5 37
George Mazarodze *v* Jeneth 1970 AAC 38 .. 58
Gibson *v* Mbishe 1949 SRN 225 81

Page

Gideon *v* Butete & Butete 1949 SRN 201 .. 39, 50
Gideon Heya *v* George Tinargwo 1973 AAC 26 .. 84
Gideon Pepukai *v* Mzanywa 1966 AAC 16 .. 34
Gilbert *v* Chandiyangana 1949 SRN 220 .. 68
Gilbert Chinogara *v* Beaula Chinogara 1970 AAC 43 64
Ginza *v* Johannes 1936 SRN 92 .. .. .. 33, 69
Gladys & Matemebele *v* Jonathan Mangwiro 1963 CAR 1 51
Godwin Mudzimu *v* Kenneth Gomwe 1975 AAC 16 .. 43, 44
Gomese *v* Agnes 1973 AAC 20 58
Grace Matumo *v* Charles Chabata 1966 AAC (ix) .. 20
Gratiano Nyangowa *v* Manenje Ndondo 1965 AAC 25 .. 37
Gunda *v* Alexander 1973 AAC 35 70
Guteyi & ors, R *v*. 1915 SR 49 43
Guwanzewe *v* Alica Murapa 1952 SRN 299 .. 16, 68

H.

Hapanshe *v* Musungwa 1970 AAC (viii) 9
Harry *v* Nomi & Esinati 1947 SRN 160 46
Haruzi Munyekete *v* Mberikwazvi Chirume 1971 AAC 27 66
Hega Kenani *v* Phillimon Chifamba 1963 CAR 44 .. 57
Henry Bwerudza *v* Samuel Muzunye Mhlanga 1959 SRN 628 77
Hlale *v* Dziyakwi 1938 SRN 34 .. .. 37, 40, 72
Hlambase *v* Wana 1937 SRN 4 59
Hlambelo *v* Dandane 1964 AAC 45 .. .. 15, 20
Hlezipe *v* Kotasi 1953 SRN 323 71
Hlomani *v* Mjayi & Mawengi 1933 SRN 53 .. 66
Honye *v* Wakayi 1955 SRN 496 38
Hope *v* Scotch 1961 SRN 19 65
Hora *v* Maendaenda 1970 AAC 13 83
Huchu *v* Magomo 1966 AAC 6 62

I.

Ida & Ben *v* Chombe 1947 SRN 151 45
Ides & Goliati *v* Getson 1963 CAR 79 67
Idi *v* Mabaza 1946 SRN 143 56
Ignatio *v* Gertrud Nkomozana 1973 AAC 15 .. 58
Ignatio Maposa *v* Gertrud Mkomozana 1975 AAC 14 31
Isaac *v* Kamoto 1953 SRN 319 32
Isaac & Peter *v* Edith & Messiah 1965 AAC 47 .. 8

Page

Isaiah Muwori *v* Petros Sabau 1867 AAC 25 45
Ishmael Ngwira *v* Mavies & Thomas Zimba 1964 AAC 22 53

J.

Jack Museyemwa *v* Samson Mupandacharo 1964 AAC 34 65
Jajina *v* Dembetembe 1963 CAR (vii) 31
Jakata *v* Kwanayi 1941 SRN 137 45
Jambawu Madondo *v* Mudzamiri 1973 AAC 24 49
James *v* Keyi 1962 SRN 16 60
James Ndava *v* Harry Chakanyuka 1968 AAC (v) .. 32
Jamu *v* Jim Takaziweyi 1939 SRN 49 .. .. 63, 81
Jane Maruta *v* Esther Katama 1969 AAC (x) 24
Japonda *v* Elisa & Jack 1945 SRN 73 47
Jarata *v* Furutsa 1947 SRN 157 47
Jema *v* David Manhare 1973 AAC 1 57
Jennifer Moya *v* Mavunga Fande 1971 AAC 21 55
Jeri *v* Saniso & Mutambiranwa 1958 SRN 579 66
Jirira *v* Jirira & anor 1976 (1) RLR (GD) 59
Job Kekana *v* Josiah Jakachira 1967 AAC 31 48
Jockoniah *v* Simanga 1967 AAC 34 65
Joel Susondo *v* Willie Rutsito 1965 AAC 8 62
Johannes Shiri *v* Mavudzi School Committee 1865 AAC 56 7
John Jack *v* Mojapelo 1965 AAC 15 .. .. 6, 23
John Paradzayi *v* Nyiwe Dzirutwe 1964 AAC 73 .. 43
John Sachikonye *v* Nyaradzai 1969 AAC 33 83
John W G Sojini *v* Jokoniah Nyati 1972 AAC 14 .. 77
Jokonya *v* Diana & Machingura 1944 SRN 44 55
Jona *Ex p.* 1954 SRN 419 31
Jona *v* Muchonisi Ernest 1954 SRN 461 36
Joseph Tinga *v* Joshua Shekede 1970 AAC 30 54
Joshua *v* Martha 1976 AAC 20 63
Joshua Murigwa *v* Johnson Mudawanhu 1970 AAC 11 .. 84
Jubajuba *v* Hendrick 1945 SRN 57 60
Julia *v* Matapulaye 1952 SRN 306 .. .. 67, 68
Juliet Munemo & Charakupa *v* Ranguta 1955 SRN 475 67
Juniah & Juniasi *v* Nawa 1949 SRN 210 .. 62, 81
Julius Makondora *v* Togarepi Nyapadzi 1967 AAC 13 .. .. 27, 33

Page

K.

Kachingwe *v* Sitima 1932 SRN 49 19
Kachiwawa, *Ex p.* 1958 SRN 545 30
Kadoho *v* Lawrence Chitsomba 1970 AAC 23 .. 37
Kaduku *v* Msodzi & Mshori 1939 SRN 56 .. 47
Kainosi *v* Tazvivinga 1973 AAC 28 70
Kamingipa *v* Jengera & Purapi 1940 SRN 92 .. .. 47, 56, 67, 71
Kangachere *v* David Khondowe 1963 CAR 33 .. 67
Kanyuka Sixpence *v* Egista a/b John Hawker 1967 AAC 37 .. .. 18, 67
Kapeta & Mairesi *v* Mugwagwa 1954 SRN 464 .. 53
Kapisi *v* Magwayi 1937 SRN 10 .. .. .. v, 60
Kapita *Ex p.* 1958 SRN 608 30
Karimbo Simon *v* David M'Wari 1974 AAC 8 .. 16
Kathleen Siwira *v* Amoni 1953 SRN 365 .. 47
Katina *v* Mutandiwa 1966 AAC 7 51
Kazire Bros. *v* T. Chihowa 1976 AAC 63 .. 8
Kechemu *v* Marisa 1953 SRN 371 22
Kefasi *v* John 1958 SRN 612 35
Kenneth *v* Enock 1963 CAR 3 28
Keresiah & Jack *v* Martha & Mugweni Makimba 1958 SRN 551 75
Khumalo S *v.* 1972 (2) RLR 415 (GD) .. 11
Komo *v* Leboho & Holmes NO 1936 SR 86 .. 79
Kufahakurotwe *v* Ajida 1966 AAC 10 .. .. 17, 65
Kufahakurotwe Simon *v* Ajida (2) 1967 AAC 42 .. 66
Kufakwedu *v* Mandizwidza 1936 SRN 85 .. 48
Kulumo *v* Diyana & others 1944 SRN 35 .. 48
Kunwanya *v* Parson NO 1972 (1) RLR 388 (GD) .. 8
Kuyu *v* Maria Moyo 1953 SRN 378 15
Kuzowomunhu *v* Eneleta & George 1949 SRN 199 .. 49

L.

Lameck Marovagondo *v* Dipa Garise 1975 AAC 38 33
Lawrence *v* Musomali 1951 SRN 259 56
Leah *v* Joshua 1932 SRN 39 50
Lenard Andina *v* Wamututu 1954 SRN 433 .. 38, 62
Leonard Ruredzo *v* Mvelase 1970 AAC 50 .. 60
Lesitoni *v* Eniyasi 1966 AAC 14 76
Leya & John Phiri *v* Masauso Banda 1958 SRN 605 53

Page

Lighton Madebgwe *v* Jamu 1964 AAC 19 .. .. 30, 31
Lovemore Mapaura *v* Erica 1970 AAC 1 31
Lucia & Chakanyuka *v* Gandizanwa 1953 SRN 388 .. 54
Lydia *v* Masumbu 1939 SRN 74 .. .. .. 64, 71

M.

Mabande *v* Masiya 1959 SRN 630 68
Mabetsu *v* Menyezwa 1944 SRN 25 33
Mabigwa *v* Matibini 1946 SRN 117 .. .. 15,59, 81
Machokomere *v* Tapfuma 1969 AAC 22 75
Mado *v* Skudamedzi 1942 SRN 193 58
Madziwa *v* Chipanda 1939 SRN 63 .. .. 40, 43
Magolis Mukogo *v* Ganganisa 1970 AAC (xi) .. 57
Magorimbo *v* Munemu 1963 CAR (viii) 16
Magret & Mangure *v* Johannes 1963 CAR 24 .. 31
Magukwa *v* Chobono 1938 SRN 31 33
Magwaro *v* Taurayi 1966 AAC 25 57
Magwegwe *v* Christopher Guni 1973 AAC (ix) .. 41
Magwisi *v* Kombayi 1947 SRN 177 .. .. .. 44, 79
Mahomedi *v* Maganga 1944 SRN 33 .. .. 16,22, 57
Maida & Stephen *v* Libona 1964 AAC 32 70
Majoni R *v*. 1963 R&N 143 (SR) 52
Majoni *v* Tawurayi 1969 AAC 16 30
Makiwa *v* Makina 1943 SRN 1 59
Mako *v* Chivadza & Kunatsa 1945 SRN 79 .. 54
Makore *v* Chikowore 1966 AAC 116 32
Makore *v* Hlupe Ignatius 1964 AAC 51 33
Malipiti & Julia *v* Kandiro 1946 SRN 94 .. 68
Mandaza *v* Tawuya Stores (Pvt) Ltd. 1963 CAR 11 8, 27
Mandiyanya Kengere *v* Musoko Muchineripi 1969 AAC 40 23
Mandizwidza *v* Tiripanu 1939 SRN 67 40
Mangwiro *v* Matema 1941 SRN 147 .. .. 19, 29
Mangwiza *v* Mwarume 1929 SRN 25 29
Manikisi *v* Sikonwane Madubege 1934 SRN 72 .. 73
Manuel *v* Karina & Nono 1964 AAC 7 65
Manuka *v* Makanyesi 1942 SRN 162 79
Manyanga *v* Matipadza & Boniface Tederere 1953 SRN 401 38
Manyore Ringi *v* Bereredzo Chimombe 1953 SRN 412 62
Maponga *Ex p*. 1958 SRN 525 30
Mapurisa *v* Tarubudira 1964 AAC (vii) .. 6

Page

Maratu *v* Mbangetwa 1941 SRN 157 40
Maredza *v* Lamuel Chiduza 1965 AAC 49 49
Maria *v* Linos 1970 AAC 46 67
Maria *v* Nyamayaro 1950 SRN 237 15
Maria & anor *v* Murimbika 1976 (1) RLR 385 (AD) 57
Marimo *v* Tasarirenamo 1957 SRN 510 39
Mariyana *v* Seven 1969 AAC 43 76
Margaret *v* Amon 1945 SRN 90 69
Martin Chaponda & Saiza *v* Piki 1964 AAC 9 .. 31
Martha Montjane *v* Levison Shumba 1977 AAC 15 .. 16
Mary & Dayiri Tom *v* Musekiwa E Gwen 1965 AAC 41 25
Mary Jenje *v* Ben Kunaka 1964 AAC (vii) 24
Mary Munjoma *v* Ferris Munjoma 1970 AAC (ix) .. 21
Marwhe & Rumane *v* Kwangwa Charlie 1957 SRN 512 .. 25
Mashako Pombe *v* Stephen Chimombe 1953 SRN 412 49,62
Mashonganyika *v* Taurayi 1966 AAC (viii) 20
Masiyiwa *v* Mchanetsa & Kasinawuyo 1938 SRN 27 .. 46
Maso *v* Nyamuya Zhuwakinyu 1971 AAC 1 57
Matambo *v* Matambo 1969 (2) RLR 154 (AD) 82
Mateko *v* Matikare 1963 CAR 57 46
Matilda Matangaidze *v* Peter Matangaidze 1972
AAC 4 27
Matiringana & Kwaramba *v* Usayi 1940 SRN 104 .. 33
Matiyenga & Mamire *v* Chinamura & ors 1958 SRN 55 76
Matsika *v* Gwama 1963 CAR 41 .. .. 7, 21
Mawaorera *v* Chavanduka 1941 SRN 119 81
Mazero *v* Farashishiko 1964 AAC (viii) 32
Mazarodze *v* Chikombe Simon 1973 AAC (iii) .. 20
Mbidzeni & Diki *v* Siya 1938 SRN 21 .. 43,46,79
Mbonisi Moyo *v* Tendayi Moyo 1976 AAC 1 .. 25,31,66
Mchenje *v* Kunaka 1912 SR 207 46
Mchemwa *v* Chandengerwa 1954 SRN 428 55
Mdujulwa *v* Madhliwa 1945 SRN 63 81
Mercy Chopamba *v* Obidiah Chopamba 1971 AAC (vi) 41
Meri *v* Merita 1966 AAC 53 35,75
Meyi Ndhlovu *v* Geula Ndhlovu 1971 AAC 22 .. 78
Mhlaba *v* Makuhlane 1947 SRN 180 82
Michael Chikololeke *v* Lameck Gabuza 1969 AAC 38 .. 71
Miki *v* Emely & Mogadzawa 1952 SRN 291 68
Mildred Mungofa *v* Julius Mungofa 1971 AAC 24 .. 65
Misaire *v* Rameki 1964 AAC (vii) 6
Misheki *v* Eniya 1960 SRN 683 17

Page

Mjaka *v* Jerimani 1946 SRN 127 53
Mkarange *v* Tamange 1949 SRN 207 69
Mkwesa *v* Maponga 1946 SRN 106 47
Mondiwo *v* Muwirimi 1952 SRN 296 55
Monica *v* Jenje Muchenje & Mbewu Tapambwa 1963 CAR 5 36
Morgen Makumbe *v* Mabugu 1965 AAC 52 77
Moses *v* Nubula & Charlton 1944 SRN 38 .. 47,69
Moses Mvenge *v* Emma Tafura 1974 AAC 9 70
Moss Boniface *v* Johannes 1961 SRN 9 60
Mota *v* Matiya 1963 CAR 26 4
Mots Kunaka *v* Phineas Chitengu 1969 AAC (v) .. 26
Moyo *v* Moyo 1959 SRN 641 81
Moyo *v* Nhlovu 1971 (2) RLR 50 (GD) 5
Mpani *v* Msetshwa 1958 SRN 557 81
Muchabayiwa *v* Emelia & Kumire 1957 SRN 520 .. 46
Muchaneta & Kanje *v* Timbe 1953 SRN 395 47
Muchechesi *v* Seven 1969 AAC 43 76
Mucheno *v* Chisamba & Chisamba 1940 SRN 27 .. 45,47,50
Mudoni *v* Felix Tutani 1955 SRN 491 38
Mugwagwa *v* Nyadlisu & Tigere 1940 SRN 106 .. 56
Muhango *v* France 1940 SRN 100 80,82
Mukarakate Chidakwa *v* Chitaukiri 1963 90 .. 51
Mukayira *v* Manuel 1966 AAC (vii) 26
Munemo *v* Mandiyera & Sengeta 1943 SRN 12 .. 55
Munetsi *v* Sarudzani a/b Miwirimi 1942 SRN 169 .. 52
Mungazi *v* Chibanda 1937 SRN 1 45,71
Munyaradzi *v* Nyunga 1975 AAC (vi) 23
Munyengetergwa *v* Katapa 1938 SRN 43 .. 33,79
Munzara *v* Muskwati 1953 SRN 402 71
Munzara *v* Nereka 1944 SRN 24 81
Murambiwa *v* Chief Nyashanu 1962 SRN 29 21
Muramwa *v* Majoni 1947 SRN 279 70
Mureza & Anna *v* Ziyai 1958 SRN 590 57
Musarurgwa *v* Magende 1959 SRN 625 83
Musekiwa Mutsonzwa *v* Big Boy a/b Kefasi Masosha 1976 AAC 38 68
Musonoki *v* Jacopo 1962 SRN 12 72
Mutandwa *v* Broko 1957 SRN 516 19
Mutetwa Johnson *v* Samson 1963 CAR 9 7
Mutizwa *Ex p.* 1958 SRN 527 31
Mutizgwa *v* Helida & Tafira 1958 SRN 565 59

Page

Mutumba R *v.* 1958 R&N 391 (SR) 52
Muwungani *v* Min. of Native Affairs 1957 R&N 298 (FSC) 2
Muza *v* Mbunjwa 1943 SRN 17 59
Muzata *v* Mahuraiswa 1966 AAC (vii) 28
Mzondiwa *v* Maguta 1947 SRN 147 15

N.

Namauzhe, Chief *v* Shumba 1975 AAC (v) 18
Naomi & Chiresi *v* Magara 1953 SRN 331 38
Nau *v* Mazwane 1946 SRN 128 82
Ndabambi *v* Raisi 1937 SRN 9 48
Ndabanengi *v* Tutai 1953 SRN 329 71
Ndhlovu *v* Sibanda 1968 (2) RLR 113 (GD) 8
Ndoro *v* Mapfumo 1942 SRN 166 40
Nelson Mutambirwa *v* Chief Soswe & others 1976 AAC 15 8
Nendaya & Tigere *v* Zidenga 1955 SRN 499 .. 44,69
Newarayi *v* Mukandah 1963 CAR (ix) 26
Newton Chimedza *v* Murindagomo 1977 AAC 17 .. 23,28
Ngonya & Gasa *v* Nyamayendga 1945 SRN 70 .. 47
Nguni *v* Sophia & Boniface 1963 CAR 28 64
Ngwabi *v* Malundu 1951 SRN 275 61
Nira *v* Marete & Ngondo 1947 SRN 175 .. iv,59
Norido *v* Hlawu Jamela 1970 AAC 16 32
Nosenga & Kefasi *v* Musadane 1954 SRN 436 .. 18
Ntubeni Bus Service *v* Vamu 1962 SRN 20 83
Nyakadzargwa *v* Lucky 1961 SRN 26 66
Nyakudja *v* Nsodzi & Mshori 1939 SRN 70 47
Nyamadzawo *v* Mandaza 1930 SRM 21 46
Nyadadzawo *v* Priska 1938 SRN 25 31
Nyamande *v* Majura Chiura 1966 AAC (xii) 34
Nyamayare *v* Chamunorgwa 1958 SRN 530 .. 75
Nyasha Raphael *v* Emily 1976 AAC 47 57
Nyatsanza *v* Frank Mandisodza 1966 AAC (xii) .. 7
Nyaumba *v* Murapa 1975 (2) RLR 138 (AD) 57
Nyengerayi *v* Sandaram 1949 SRN 205 .. 44,60
Nyoni *v* Mamova 1949 SRN 216 62,72
Nyovane *v* Murongwana 1956 SRN 503 75
Nzira & Chitimbe *v* Zwinavashe 1947 SRN 161 .. 29,66
Nzuwa *v* Mark Makuwa 1971 AAC 39 60

Page

P.

Paradza Chibova *v* Tatayi Museve 1964 AAC 4 .. 22
Pasco Nyamariwa Gunda (and Mr Mkushi) *v* Margaret Faina & Boniface Monyani 1976 AAC 31 59
Patsika *Ex p.* 1954 SRN 435 31
Paul Masembura *v* Juawo Yawo 1972 AAC 28 36
Pemha *v* Joshua Patrick Zwichemo 1972 AAC 9 .. 27,65
Percy Budiyo *v* Peter Chimivedzi 1974 AAC 13 .. 60
Percy & Emily Mukumbe *v* Maria 1969 AAC (x) .. 32
Peter Ntenetzi *v* Timothy Mapango 1965 AAC 36 .. 22,35
Petros Sithole *v* Moses Rukunda 1976 AAC 6 .. 31,59
Philimon Mpofu *v* Solomon & Edith 1969 AAC (viii) 54
Pikani Simeon *v* Patrick Gufu 1959 SRN 620 .. 78
Pisira *v* Enoki Sonokele 1954 SRN 446 29,82
Portopiro *v* Samson Burangwa 1964 AAC 11 .. 66
Potiphar Munkodya *v* Chinganga David 1971 AAC 2 .. 28
Prisca *v* Mutandizi Maxwell Makwara 1976 AAC 9 .. 78
Puce *v* Sandalamu 1943 SRN 14 29,37
Purazi Chipfaracha *v* Chris 1972 AAC (vii) .. 18

R.

Rabecca & Musiyima *v* Vurayayi 1958 SRN 571 .. 59
Rabson *v* Makoti 1969 AAC 54 77
Raphael Moyo *v* Mugwagwa Moyo 1977 AAC 5 .. 20
R *v* Chokumarara 1945 SR 88 52
R *v* Guteyi & others 1915 SR 49 43
R *v* Majoni 1963 R&N 143 (SR) 52
R *v* Mutumba 1958 R&N 391 (SR) 52
R *v* Ngono et uxor 1915 SR 1 53
Reuben Mhlanga *v* Mabula Masuku 1967 AAC 9 .. 22
Reya & Kapita *v* Zuze 1951 SRN 269 53
Rhodia *v* Mandala 1942 SRN 179 53
Richard Mpofu *v* Daisy Dube a/b Hambe Dube 1967 AAC 21 77
Richard Shumba *v* Tsakayirenzi 1973 AAC 7 .. 84
Ringirai *v* Changara 1970 AAC 9 83
Rison *v* Jeremiah 1958 SRN 526 50
Robert *in re* 1953 SR 47 70
Robert Abraham 1952 SRN 293 70
Robert *v* Mugwagwa 1954 SRN 458 37
Roseman Dlamini *v* Kariot Mtambo 1971 AAC (vi) .. 25
Ruben Zimbura *v* Josiah 1966 AAC (xiv) 37

Page

Rudia & Enock *v* Ignatius Rangarirayi 1964 AAC 66 75
Ruka *v* Pfidze 1963 CAR 47 36
Ruka *v* Tose 1946 SRN 82 61
Rusiya a/b Samuel *v* Lucy a/b Banwell 1954 SRN 455 59
Russell Samuriwo *v* Robson Dhlamini 1975 AAC 9 .. 27
Ruwo *v* Rabson 1965 AAC 20 76

S.

Saida *v* David 1965 AAC 38 56
Sam Msonko *v* Mutuswu 1963 CAR 7 69
Samanyika Mwale *v* Mangwiro 1955 SRN 493 .. 38
Sambo *v* Moyo & Makumalo 1939 SRN 58 .. 16,44,73
Samson *v* Justin 1952 SRN 344 81
Samuel *v* Chimugarwe 1969 AAC 4 57
Samuel Ntuli *v* Simon Mlambo 1970 AAC (xii) .. 35
Samuel Shumba *v* Johnson 1973 AAC 3 .. 27,34,36
Sandi Chikomba Chikungwana *v* Wunganai Chiutso 1975 AAC 22 19
Sangirayi *v* Zingowa 1938 SRN 37 .. 45,50
Sanislayi *v* Sophia & Jackson 1951 SRN 279 .. 70
Seti & others, *Ex p.* 1963 R&N 681 (SR) 63
Sevi & Ginatsio *v* Robert 1958 SRN 562 43
Shadreck Chitima *v* Gideon Danatu 1962 SRN 27 .. 59
Shambara Washeya *v* Chief Dandawa 1975 AAC 25 .. 6,16
Shangwa *v* Jona Virimayi 1969 AAC 45 77
Sheneti *v* Sadosa 1961 SRN 15 72
Sheriwa *v* Risi & Mubayiwa 1944 SRN 27 55
Shingirayi *v* Chiwonesu 1953 SRN 342 .. 47,67
Shonai *v* Nyamfarira 1941 SRN 132 48
Shoniwa *v* Jameson 1950 SRN 238 39,58
Shoniwa *v* Jenje 1958 SRN 543 38
Shoniwa Rackswell Chinamano *v* Mariyoti Gurajena 1974 AAC 3 65
Shumba *v* Tichareva 1958 SRN 547 38
Siamosa *v* Kadembo 1953 SRN 325 70
Sigonqo *v* Matombi & Pameti 1958 SRN 855 .. 46,53
Sigumila *v* Ben Sibanda 1964 AAC 48 39
Simbodza *v* Maviyo 1955 SRN 782 67
Simon Machongwe *v* Christine Farusa 1972 AAC 21 58
Simon *v* Manukusa 1946 SRN 132 62
Simon Moyo *v* Mawere Mapetere 1974 AAC 11 .. 60

Page

Simon Ndhlovu *v* Edward 1973 AAC (viii) 35
Simon *v* Puweyi & Takaidza 1964 AAC 1 46
Sipamehle *v* Dube 1940 SRN 79 81
Sitayi *v* Lomacala & Mhlahla 1930 SRN 33 29
Siyamakayi *v* Tawodzera 1934 SR 68 46
Stanley Machakanja *v* Martin 1963 CAR 19 39
S *v* Khumalo 1972 (2) RLR 415 (GD) 11
S *v* Takaendisa 1972 (1) RLR 375 (AD) 2
Stewart a/b Patrick *v* Chigumbura 1971 AAC 35 .. 76
Swondo *v* Gombingo 1967 AAC 16 77

T.

Tabana *v* Gumani 1962 SRN 23 62
Tabita & Jasi *v* Tawonezwi 1961 SRN 33 64
Tabitha Chiduku *v* Chidano 1922 SR 55 5,65
Tabiya & Sineki *v* Nyama 1963 CAR 15 .. 39,67
Tafirenyika *Ex p.* 1954 SRN 454 31
Tafirenyika *v* Esther 1965 AAC (vii) 24
Takaendisa, S *v.* 1972 (1) RLR 375 (AD) .. 2
Takawadiyi *v* Munyukwi Siyawamwuya 1969 AAC 47 .. 76
Tamayi Moyo *v* Maqude Kabo 1966 AAC (xi) 21
Tambi *v* Sailos 1953 SRN 346 47,62
Tambudzayi *v* Samuriwo 1976 (1) RLR 27 (AD).. 13,17,29
Tandiwa *v* Muchaneta & Chingombe 1965 AAC 59 .. 47
Tangwara *v* Tlili 1960 SRN 680 83
Tapera Chikunga *v* Muhambi Jack 1964 AAC 70 .. 23
Tapfumaneyi Alexander *v* Tandiwe Musayeya 1973 AAC 17 54
Taruwinga *v* Mrewa 1941 SRN 154 22
Tasara *v* Agnes Manjaya 1958 SRN 581 15
Tasara Antonio *v* Romos 1962 SRN 1 77
Tasarirobona Mrindi *v* Turi 1967 AAC 28 43
Tasiyana *v* Meriya 1969 AAC 76 55
Tawonerera *v* Matenzeyi & Muchabayiwa 1953 SRN 359 38
Tawonezwi *v* Taziwinga 1957 SRN 518 38
Terera *v* Sithole & Sithole 1964 AAC 38 77
Teresa & Gwabanai *v* Akupusa 1958 SRN 549 .. 47
Thom *v* Raina & Ben 1952 SRN 294 53
Thomas *v* Josiah 1959 SRN 655 51
Tigere & Hana *v* Dick Chokumarara 1963 CAR 35 35
Tiki Parima Makuni *v* Nyandora Jairos 1970 AAC 22 38

Page

Tinapi *v* Chiwenga 1938 SRN 45 33
Tinavapi Machinjike *v* Bunhu Mujikwa 1969 AAC 78 48
Titus Dube *v* Munyoro William 1971 AAC 6 .. 83
Tobias Gudidu *v* Kenneth Mapungani 1965 AAC 12 .. 58
Tobias Madondoro *v* Dapi Chirwa 1970 AAC 19 .. 37
Tobias *v* Mandizwidza 1968 AAC 7 65
Tokorekoria *v* Patrick Mtutu 1953 SRN 384 .. 62
Tolongo *v* Mbasela 1944 SRN 41 40
Tondhlana & Dhliwayo *v* Tondhlana 1964 AAC (viii) 51
Try Again Bus Service & Semu Moyo NO *v* James Moyo 1964 AAC 26 78
Tsaurayi *v* Parunobva 1960 SRN 674 18
Tsikayi *Ex p.* 1959 SRN 619 31

U.

Usanga *Ex p.* 1955 SRN 485 30
Useni *v* Zhuwakinyu 1953 SRN 386 58

V.

Vela *v* Mondinika & Maguta 1936 SRN 171 .. 71
Venancio Musiyiwa Muzenda *v* Timothy T Mtengwe 1972 AAC (vi) 32
Violet & Mahlaule *v* Girison 1964 AAC 43 .. 76
Vobe Jere *v* Chadeura Gamaliel & Jairos Gungu 1959 SR 652 4

W.

Wafani *v* Nyoni 1962 SRN 25 60
William Join *v* Regina Chiyaka a/b Chinyama 1967 AAC 24 35
Willie *v* Mapfumo 1950 SRN 244 39
Willie *v* Matafi 1941 SRN 126 82
Wilson Mataga *v* Eriza & Mutandwa 1953 SRN 391 .. 54
Wiston Chikuwe *v* Nyanzira 1964 AAC 41 .. 60

Y.

Yotam *Ex p.* 1947 SRN 176 30
Youngs Mlalazi *v* John 1969 AAC 14 28

Page

Z.

Zakaria Rusere *v* Tambaureyi Newman 1969 AAC 18 .. 34
Zakiya & two others *v* Tavarwisa & Pomeryai 1971 AAC 11 28
Zihumbga *v* Harper NO & others 1965 RLR 382 (GD) 2,8
Zimunu *v* Chakawarika 1933 SRN 60 40
Zira *v* Pompey 1946 SRN 137 69
Zwomazva *v* Josephine 1973 AAC 22 48

CHAPTER 1

GENERAL PRINCIPLES OF APPLICATION AND JURISDICTION

A. ASCERTAINMENT AND APPLICATION

B. JURISDICTION OF COURTS

A. ASCERTAINMENT AND APPLICATION

Definitions

'Customary law', in relation to a particular African tribe, means the legal principles and judicial practices of such tribe except in so far as such principles or practices are repugnant to -

(a) natural justice or morality; or

(b) the provisions of any enactment:

Provided that nothing in any enactment relating to the age of majority, the status of women, the effect of marriage on the property of the spouses, the guardianship of children or the administration of deceased estates, shall affect the application of customary law, except in so far as such enactment has been specifically applied to Africans by that or any other enactment - *vide* section 2 of the African Law and Tribal Courts Act *(Chapter 237)*.

'African' means -

(a) any member of the aborginal tribes or races of Africa and the islands adjacent thereto, including Madagascar and Zanzibar; or

(b) any person who has the blood of such tribes or races and who lives as a member of an aboriginal native community - *vide* section 3 of the Interpretation Act *(Chapter 1)*.

'Tribe' means a number or collection of Africans forming an organization or community under the control or leadership of a chief - *vide* section 2 of the African Affairs Act *(Chapter 228)*. The old native tribal system has long since disappeared and the composition of a tribe is wholly determined by administrative decisions made under the laws of the country - *Muwuungani* v *The Minister of Native Affairs* 1957 R&N 298 (FSC). A tribe does not possess a corporate personality and is not capable of acquiring rights or incurring obligations or of suing in its own name - *Zihumbga* v *Harper NO & others* 1965 RLR 382 (GD).

'Enactment' means any Act, any statute included in a Revised Edition of the Statute Laws of Rhodesia prepared under an Act, any statutory instrument, any regulations made in terms of an Order in Council made under the Federation of Rhodesia and Nyasaland Act 1963, of the United Kingdom, or any provision contained in any enactment - *vide* section 3 of the Interpretation Act *(Chapter 1)*.

'Chief' means an African appointed by the President to exercise control over a tribe as chief, acting chief or deputy of a chief - *vide* section 2 of the African Affairs Act *(Chapter 228)*. A customary interim tribal head, while he may under customary law perform some of the functions of a chief, has no statutory authority as a chief - *S* v *Takaendisa* 1972 (1) RLR 325 (AD).

Ascertainment

If the court is in any doubt as to the existence or content of a rule of customary law, it is expressly provided in section 5 of the African Law and Tribal Courts Act *(Chapter 237)* that, having considered such submissions thereon as may be made by or on behalf of the parties, it may consult reported cases, textbooks and other sources, and, to enable it to arrive at a decision in the matter, may receive opinions either orally or in writing, including expert evidence to show that customs have changed over the years - *Everest Dube* v *Chief Myinga* 1965 AAC 1. Provided that after hearing such submissions or oral opinion, the decision made shall be one for the court. Moreover, any reported cases, textbooks and opinions consulted by the court shall be made available to the parties.

Application

Subject to the provisions of certain statutory limitations, in the determination by any court of law of any civil case between Africans or between an African and a person who is not an African the decision may be given in accordance with customary law - section 3(1) of the African Law and Tribal Courts Act *(Chapter 237)*.

In consequence of the provisions of this section, customary law is applicable in any case which is between Africans and which relates to -

(a) seduction or adultery;

(b) the custody or guardianship of children: Provided that in relation to the custody of children, the interests of such children shall be the paramount consideration;

(c) the devolution otherwise than by will or movable property on the death of an African, except where the deceased was an African mentioned in section 69 of the Administration of Estates Act *(Chapter 301) (infra)*, when the provisions of that section shall apply;

(d) rights in land which is not held under individual registered title;

(e) marriage consideration;

(f) a marriage between Africans contracted under customary law, whether or not it has been solemnized under the African Marriages Act *(Chapter 238)*.

In any other case, the law of Rhodesia shall apply.

The law of Rhodesia also applies to the determination of the capacity of an African to enter into any transaction or to enforce or defend any rights in a court of law, subject to any enactment affecting such capacity - section 3(2) of the African Law and Tribal Courts Act *(Chapter 237)*. However, this provision has no application if the existence or extent of any right which is held or alleged to be held by an African or of any obligation vesting or alleged to be vesting in any African depends upon or is governed by customary law. In which case, the capacity of the African concerned in relation to any matter affecting that right or obligation is governed by customary law.

In general, and always subject to any enactment, if it appears from express or tacit agreement of the parties, or from express consent of the parties, or from the nature or circumstances surrounding the matter within which any case has arisen it can be presumed the parties have agreed, customary law or, as the case may be, the law of Rhodesia is applicable - section 3(3) of the African Law and Tribal Courts Act *(Chapter 237)*. In this section, by 'the law of Rhodesia' is meant the common law.

In any case where the parties are connected with different tribes with different systems of customary law, the court shall apply the customary law by which the parties agreed or may be presumed to have agreed that their obligations should be regulated or, in the absence of such actual or presumed agreement, the customary law of the place where the cause of action arose - section 4 of the African Law and Tribal Courts Act *(Chapter 237)*.

In cases where no express rule is applicable, or if there is no customary law of that place or it is not ascertainable, the court shall apply the principles of justice, equity and good conscience - sections 3(4) & 4 of the African Law and Tribal Courts Act *(Chapter 237)*. The policy is to apply customary law unless there is some definite reason to the contrary - *Duma* v *Madidi* 1918 SR 59. In pursuance of general policy, however, prescription applies to customary law whether or not it is a principle thereof - *Vobe Jere* v *Chadzura Gamaliel & Jairos Gungu* 1959 SRN 652 -- but it must be pleaded - *Mota* v *Matiya* 1963 CAR 26.

Subject to the provisions of any enactment, the most cogent reason for not applying customary law is that such law is repugnant to natural justice or morality, as that phrase is used in the definition of customary law *(supra)*. What may constitute the principles or practices which are repugnant to natural justice or morality will depend on the particular circumstances in which the issue is raised. However, in *Tabitha Chiduku* v *Chidano* 1922 SR 55, Tredgold SJ considered that they should apply only to such customs as inherently impress the court with some abhorrence or which are obviously immoral in their incidence. It is submitted that this is the logical and most practical test to apply. See also *Chakawa* v *Goro* 1959 (1) R&N 188 (NACSR).

B. JURISDICTION OF COURTS

High Court of Rhodesia

In terms of subsection (8) of section 6 of the African Affairs Act *(Chapter 228)* an appeal from the Court of Appeal for African Civil Cases lies to the Appellate Division of the High Court. The procedure applicable in relation to such appeals may be found in the High Court (Appellate Division) (Miscellaneous Appeals and References) Rules 1975, published in Rhodesia Government Notice 449 of 1975.

Subject to the provisions of section 24 of the African Law and Tribal Courts Act *(Chapter 237)* relating to criminal cases, the General Division of the High Court exercises no jurisdiction in customary law - *Moyo* v *Ndhlovu* 1971 (2) RLR 50 (GD).

Court of Appeal for African Civil Cases

Subsection (1) of section 6 of the African Affairs Act *(Chapter 228)* provides for the constitution of a Court of Appeal for the purpose of hearing appeals from the court of a district commissioner. The court consists of three members of whom one shall be appointed as president by the Minister of Justice - section 6(2) of the Act. The other members of the court are selected by the president from a list of persons nominated by the Minister of Internal Affairs who are, or have been, district commissioners or native commissioners - section 4(4) of the Act. The president shall be a former judge of the High Court, a judge or former judge of the Water Court, a person who is and has been for not less than ten years qualified to practise as an advocate in Rhodesia or a person who has been a magistrate for not less than ten years - section 6(3) of the Act.

The Court of Appeal may sit in such places as the president of the court may determine - section 6(6) of the Act.

Any decision of the majority of the Court of Appeal shall be the decision of the court, and the court shall possess the same powers in respect of appeals from the court of a district commissioner as are exercisable by the Appellate Division of the High Court in appeals from magistrates' courts. The rules of the court may be found in the Court of Appeal for Native Civil Cases Rules 1960, published in Rhodesia Government Notice 116 of 1960 (Appendix II).

The Court of Appeal is a creature of statute and derives its jurisdiction and power from the statute and nowhere else. In consequence it has no inherent jurisdiction - *John Jack* v *Mojapelo* 1965 AAC 15. It cannot, for example, entertain claims at law relating to administrative matters, such as the creation of a kraal - *Practice Note: Mapurisa* v *Tarubudira* 1964 AAC (vii), or the transfer of grazing rights - *Practice Note: Misaire* v *Rameki* 1964 AAC (vii). Although it may hear an appeal against judgment in a dispute as to who should be headman of a kraal, notwithstanding that this is more properly an administrative matter - *Chikandiwa* v *Kraalhead Masiya* 1973 AAC 11. Neither has it any powers of review - *Practice Note: Davius* v *Tigere* 1967 AAC (viii), or the power to interfere with the decision of a tribal court, although it may be able to take certain administrative action in an endeavour to correct the proceedings - *Shambare Washaya* v *Chief Dandawa* 1975 AAC 25.

The court has a discretion to make any order as to costs, and right of audience is extended to advocates and attorneys of the High Court.

Courts of District Commissioners

A district commissioner may hold a court, which is a court of record, in such place or places within his district as seem to him most suitable, for the purpose either of trying civil suits in which the rights of

Africans only are concerned or which have been transferred from a magistrates court, in terms of the Magistrates' Court Act *(Chapter 18)* - section 5 of the African Affairs Act *(Chapter 228)*.

A district commissioner's court is limited in its jurisdiction by application of the provisions of paragraph (b) of subsection (1) of section 13 of the Magistrates' Court Act *(Chapter 18)* which apply to it. This provision largely concerns the financial jurisdiction of the court, wherein actions in relation to liquid documents are limited to a value of two thousand dollars plus interest, and in actions for delivery of property, ejectment, and all other claims to one thousand dollars, whether the property concerned in a particular action is movable or immovable. However, claims may depend on a number of different causes of action, and only to the extent to which claims depending in a particular cause exceed the jurisdiction is the jurisdiction of the court exceeded - *Practice Note: C S Nyatsanza* v *Frank Mandisodza* 1966 AAC (xii); *contra: Mutetwa Johnson* v *Samson* 1963 CAR 9; *Matsike* v *Gwama* 1963 CAR 41. If it is intended to abandon part of a claim in order to bring it within the court's jurisdiction, then this must be done *ex facie* the summons and cannot be done subsequently or by amendment of the summons - *Johannes Shiri* v *Mavudzi School Committee* 1965 AAC 56. And the proper time for such abandonment is at the start of the proceedings - *Mutetwa Johnson's* case *(supra)*.

The jurisdiction of a district commissioner's court is further limited, notwithstanding that the matter is to be decided by customary law, in disputes concerning the devolution of property of a deceased's estate to which the provisions of section 69 of the Administration of Estates Act *(Chapter 301)* apply. In such cases the jurisdiction of a district commissioner is ousted and, in such cases, expressly conferred upon the provincial or senior magistrate of the province in which the deceased ordinarily resided at the time of his death, and any appeal from the decision of the magistrate lies not to the Court of Appeal for African Civil Cases but to the Appellate Division of the High Court, in terms of subsections

(2) to (4) of that section - *Isaac & Peter* v *Edith & Messiah* 1965 AAC 47.

The court of a district commissioner may be assisted by a chief, who sits and acts as assessor, to advise on any matter concerning African law and custom. Such a court is empowered to make orders as to costs, and right of audience is extended to advocates and attorneys of the High Court. The court must be properly constituted and regularly conducted, although an *ex parte* application may be heard in a district commissioner's office if there is no prejudice to the parties - *Ndhlovu* v *Sibanda* 1968 (2) RLR 113 (GD). And when the court sits due notice must be given to all interested parties - *Kunkwenya* v *Parsons NO* 1972 (1) RLR 388 (GD).

In any matter relating to the custody or maintenance of a child the court has the power, by issue of a subpoena addressed to the person having possession or control of the child, to order and require such person to produce the child before it.

For the purpose of the exercise of the jurisdiction of a district commissioner's court subsection (6) of section 5 of the African Affairs Act *(Chapter 228)* provides that the term 'African' shall include any company or body of persons, corporate or unincorporate, if the persons who have a controlling interest therein are Africans, and a provincial authority, African council or tribal land authority. (This provision overrules the finding in *Mandaza* v *Tawuya Stores (Pvt) Ltd* 1963 CAR 11.) (A tribal land authority is concerned with giving authority for the occupancy of land and it is not empowered to settle disputes arising from such occupation. These should be settled in court in the ordinary way - *Kazire Brothers* v *T Chihowa* 1976 AAC 63.) It does not, however, grant *locus standi* to a tribe as being a corporate entity - *Zihumbga* v *Harper NO & others* 1965 RLR 382 (GD). In a dispute between a chief and a headman or kraalhead, a district commissioner should not in his judicial capacity make a declaratory order unless it will serve an effective purpose. The proper method is to act in his administrative capacity - *Nelson Mutambirwa* v *Chief Soswe & others* 1976 AAC 15.

In the case of proceedings by or against the committee of an association, it is irregular to cite the chairman alone. All the members of the committee should be joined - *Practice Note: Hapanshe* v *Musungwa* 1970 AAC (viii).

Tribal Courts

Part II of the African Law and Tribal Courts Act *(Chapter 237)* provides for the constitution of tribal courts by warrant under the hand of a person authorized thereto by the Minister of Internal Affairs. Once constituted in this manner such a court is a court of law exercising the jurisdiction conferred by the Act. Criminal jurisdiction may not be exercised by a tribal court without the approval of the Minister of Justice. The warrant constituting the court specifies the territorial limits of jurisdiction and the chief or headman appointed as the president thereof. Unless special provision is made in the warrant the appointment of the court's president is vested *ex officio* in the person of the holder of the office of the chief or headman concerned. The president exercises all the jurisdiction and powers of the court but when hearing a case must be assisted by not less than two assessors, chosen by him in accordance with custom.

The provincial commissioner is empowered to suspend any of the powers conferred in the warrant if he is of the opinion that those powers are being abused by the president of the court, or if the president conducts himself in a manner inconsistent with the discharge of his duties.

A properly constituted headman's court may at any stage before judgment, either of its own motion or at the request of a party to the proceedings, stop the proceedings and transfer the case to the chief's court, or to the court of another headman with competent jurisdiction under the same chief. In this event, the proceedings shall be deemed to have been annulled and the court to which the matter is transferred shall be deemed to have the same territorial jurisdiction as the original court. If a request is made by a party to the proceedings for transfer to a chief's court, the court of a headman has no power to refuse the request. Transfer in similar manner may, *mutatis mutandis*, be made at any time after judgment, but with the limitation that such transfer be made only to a chief's court and not to that of another headman.

A tribal court exercises jurisdiction, subject to the provisions of the Act, in any civil case in which customary law is applicable, between Africans where the defendant normally resides within the area of jurisdiction of the court or the cause of action or any element thereof arose in that area or the defendant consents to the jurisdiction of the court, or, in similar circumstances, between an African and a person who is not an African, if the latter consents to the jurisdiction of the court. Any consent given must be in writing and forms a part of the court record of the case. A tribal court is empowered to determine actions relating to marriage consideration - *lobolo* - or incidental obligations arising from a marriage which has been dissolved by another court, but has no jurisdiction to dissolve a marriage contracted under the Marriages Act *(Chapter 37)*. Tribal courts are under the direct supervision of the district commissioner in whose district they are established.

Any party who is dissatisfied with a judgment or order of a chief's court may appeal to a tribal appeal court. Such an appeal court is constituted by warrant under the hand of the Minister of Internal Affairs. A tribal appeal court is established by the appointment of four or more chiefs who are presidents of tribal courts in any one province, as members of a tribal appeal court. Three chiefs shall constitute a quorum in such a court. The court has power to hear and determine any appeal to it from a chief's court and its decision in any matter, other than a removal order, is final and not subject to further appeal.

Except in accordance with, or required or permitted by customary law, no party may be represented by any other person in a tribal court or tribal appeal court.

A chief who has no warrant issued for the establishment of a tribal court whereby he exercises any judicial function in terms of the Act may, nevertheless, if he does in fact hold a 'court' or *dare* to hear complaints made to him, be held to be acting as an arbitrator. As such, his conduct cannot be said to be the exercise of judicial functions because the exercise of such functions is circumscribed by the Act. However, this does not necessarily mean that by acting as an arbitrator his conduct is unlawful – *S* v *Khumalo* 1972 (2) RLR 415 (GD).

CHAPTER II

PROCEDURE AND EVIDENCE

A. PROCEDURE IN DISTRICT COMMISSIONERS' COURTS

Section 1. *Commencement of Proceedings*

Section 2. *Conduct of Proceedings*

Section 3. *Judgment and Appeal*

B. PROCEDURE IN THE COURT OF APPEAL

C. EVIDENCE

A. PROCEDURE IN DISTRICT COMMISSIONERS' COURTS

General

The whole object of setting up district commissioners' courts is to provide a court with a simple procedure, in which court Africans might have their civil cases determined with a minimum of formality. Although a case starts by the issue of a summons in which the plaintiff sets out what his complaint is, there are virtually no pleadings and in the trial of these cases, the district commissioner's court should not, therefore, consider itself bound in any way by the pleadings. The first duty of such a court is to try to ascertain as best it can what the precise issues between the parties are, and it should not consider itself to be rigidly bound by the complaint as it appears in the summons. Once this has been ascertained it should be explained to the parties and recorded in writing. If it then appears to the court that there is no substance to the complaint the matter should be determined forthwith and the reasons for the court's decision recorded. If, on the other hand, the court is satisfied the parties are prepared to proceed the district commissioner should forthwith try all the issues raised, and thereafter give reasons for his judgment - *Tambudzayi* v *Samuriwo* 1976 (1) RLR 27 (AD).

(1) COMMENCEMENT OF PROCEEDINGS

Receiving of Claims

A claim is lodged with the clerk of the district commissioner's court which has jurisdiction to hear the matter, at a place determined by the district commissioner, during normal office hours. When a claim is lodged and the appropriate fee tended, the clerk of court is responsible for drawing up a summons and recording the address for service of documents on both parties - rule 3 of the District Commissioner's Court Rules 1973.

In general, while no specified form of summons is required, the object is to put the defendant in full possession of the facts alleged in the plaintiff's claim - *Practice Note: Enita Marechera a/b Jeremiah Marechera* v *Naome Chidziva a/b Chamundorwa Martin Chidziva* 1969 AAC (ix). It is thus necessary to particularize sufficiently to enable the defendant to know what case he has to meet - *Swondo* v *Gombingo* 1967 AAC 16. For in the absence of such information the defendant might be severely prejudiced in the preparation of his defence, as it would only be once the evidence had been given in court that he would know the material facts upon which the plaintiff is relying. The fact that an application might be made for further and better particulars is not a satisfactory reason for not giving them in the first place - *Practice Note: Alick* v *Solomon* 1967 AAC (viii).

After he has drawn up the summons for the plaintiff, the clerk of court fixes a date, time and place for hearing the claim and notifies the plaintiff accordingly - rule 4.

Notice to Defendant

The messenger of court, that is to say, a messenger (usually referred to as a *chikonzi* or *sikonzi*) appointed by the district commissioner, then serves the summons on the defendant, warning him that the address where service is effected will be taken as the address for service of other documents, unless he notifies the clerk of court to the contrary within seven days. As far as practicable the messenger shall inform the defendant of the nature and grounds of the claim, and the place and time of hearing, ensuring that he knows that the defendant is required to appear with his witnesses - rule 5(1)(2).

As soon as service has been effected, the messenger must enter a return of service to the clerk of court - rule 5(3). If a messenger certifies that he has made personal service when in fact service has been upon a relative of the defendant, or by some other means, and he is a messenger who is known to be acquainted with the duties of a messenger, so that his transgression is wilful and likely to deceive, he should not be called upon to officiate again - *Cyril Mangwanda* v *Frank Mbanje* 1961 SRN 936.

A defendant may consent to judgment on the full amount of the claim against him by either signing the form of consent on the original summons or notifying the clerk of court before the time appointed for the hearing - rule 5(4).

Securing the attendance of witnesses

The attendance of a witness is by subpoena, served by the messenger, issued at the instance of the party requiring his attendance - rule 6(1)(2).

Service of documents and process

If personal service of any document cannot be effected, the district commissioner may instruct that it should be served in any manner provided for in terms of section 34 of the Interpretation Act *(Chapter 1)* and if this is unsatisfactory service may be by advertisement - rule 7.

When the person to be served with process cannot be found at the place chosen by him as *domicilium citandi*, and there is no one there who represents him or is willing and able to accept process, service may only validly be effected there by leaving the process affixed to some part of the premises such as the front door or wall or gate post, where it will be readily visible. It is the messenger's duty to select an appropriate part of the premises on which to post up the notice - *Crispen Makugutu* v *Peter Sibanda* 1966 AAC 15.

(2) CONDUCT OF PROCEEDINGS

Representation of parties

Any party to a case may be represented by an advocate or attorney of the High Court - rule 8(1).

If a party dies or, in the opinion of the court, is incompetent to continue an action, the action shall be stayed until such time as the court is satisfied that there is an heir, guardian or other competent person to take over the legal responsibilities of such party, or until such incompetence ceases to exist - rule 8(2).

In general, an African woman has no *locus standi in judicio* and must be assisted by her guardian - *Hlambelo* v *Dandane* 1964 AAC 45; *Maria* v *Nyamayaro* 1950 SRN 237. However, this is not always the case; and a widow may sue unassisted to protect her husband's estate - *Mabigwa* v *Matibini* 1946 SRN 117 - and a divorcee of a Christian marriage must herself sue for the return of her property - *Mzondiwa* v *Maguta* 1947 SRN 147. Moreover, a woman carrying on business as a licensed trader may sue or be sued unassisted in respect of actions arising from her business - *Tasara* v *Agnes Manjaya* 1958 SRN 581. In such a case, however, she must show that she has such a right and failure to do so will mean that the original case will be set aside and the case dismissed, leaving it for the plaintiff to bring fresh proceedings properly assisted by her guardian - *Hlambelo's* case *(supra)*; *Kuyu* v *Maria Moyo* 1953 SRN 375; *Elizabeth Makola* v *Gondongwe* 1954 SRN 407. Where a woman has no *locus standi*, the proper procedure is to cite her as 'assisted by' her guardian and, if she is the defendant in the action, to serve the summons on the guardian as well as on the woman. Then, at the outset of the trial, the presiding officer should satisfy himself that she is properly assisted. This procedure should also be followed in any notice of appeal - *Practice Note: Elizabeth* v *Enelda a/b John Zachasy* 1966 AAC (xiv).

When the paternity of the child of an unmarried woman is in issue, her guardian should be joined with her as a party - *Sambo* v *Moyo and Makumalo* 1939 SRN 58. And in actions for adultery against a married woman, the proper person to sue is the woman's husband, her brother or natural guardian has no *locus standi* - *Mahomedi* v *Maganga* 1944 SRN 33.

The mother of a minor child has no *locus standi* and the child should be assisted by a male relative - *David Moyo a/b Baita* v *Richard* 1953 SRN 327 - that is, someone who is the guardian of the minor - *Shambare Washaya* v *Chief Dandawa* 1975 AAC 25; *Martha Montjane* v *Levison Shumba* 1977 AAC 15. The father of an emancipated child, who is living apart from his parents, is married and supporting his own household, has no *locus standi* to represent his son in legal proceedings - *Karimbo Simon* v *David M'wari* 1974 AAC 8.

Record of proceedings

In every case the proceedings shall be recorded in writing and the presiding officer shall note all the relevant facts and objections which either party may desire to be recorded - rule 9(1). Verbatim answers noted in the record, to questions which are not recorded, can sometimes be meaningless. It is important, therefore, that evidence should be recorded in such a way that when the record is read thereafter the substance of a witness's evidence is properly disclosed - *Practice Note: Magorimbo* v *Munemu* 1963 CAR (viii). In suits concerning children, the name, age and sex of each child must be recorded - *Guwanzewe* v *Alice and Murapa* 1952 SRN 299 - and in awarding the custody of children the judgment should state clearly the names and ages of the children and the dates on which custody begins and ends - *Elisa and Musonda* v *Lavu* 1949 SRN 228. The proceedings in court may be conducted in whatever language is most conducive to the interests of justice but the record must be kept in English - rule 9(2)(3).

Following the decision in *Chiduku* v *Samiyele* 1944 SRN 23, when terms in the vernacular are used the English equivalent should be noted. This does not mean that a translation is required in every case. Where such terms are recognized as being of common usage in custom, for example, the term *lobolo*, then a translation is not required. Words that have already been accepted in their meaning in recognized customs or in decided cases or in both need not be translated to offer guidance to the Court of Appeal as to their meaning - *Practice Note: Misheki* v *Eniya* 1960 SRN 683.

Reading of the claim

If the claim has not been withdrawn or satisfied by the defendant consenting to judgment, the presiding officer shall bring on the case at the time appointed, or as soon as is convenient - rule 10(1). Thereafter, the court shall ask the plaintiff if he agrees to the terms of the claim or if he wants it to be amended - rule 10(2)(*a*). The ordinary rules of pleadings are not applied with strictness in district commissioners' courts, and the court is entitled to go beyond the strict confines of the claim - *Gatsi* v *Dokari* 1932 SRN 51. Nevertheless, no amendment should be made to a summons which has been served on the defendant without giving him an opportunity of being heard and it should be recorded whether he consents or not to the alteration. The reasons therefor should be stated and the amendment initialled - *Kufahakurotwe* v *Ajida* 1966 AAC 10. This should not inhibit the court from making an appropriate amendment, for the court should be able to determine the real issues and should not attach overmuch importance to the technicalities of precise pleadings, provided that the parties are not prejudiced. Cases in front of district commissioners should be determined with the minimum amount of formality in an attempt to resolve the real issues between the parties - *Tambudzayi* v *Samuriwo* 1976 (1) RLR 27 (AD).

The claim should then be put to the defendant - rule 10(2) (b) and his attitude recorded - rule 10(2)(e); *Tsaurayi* v *Parunobva* 1960 SRN 674; *Practice Note: Chimbi* v *Chitumba* 1975 AAC (v). If the presiding officer entertains any doubts as to the accuracy of the defendant plea, he should not let the trial continue but must satisfy himself by questioning the defendant, to ascertain exactly what he meant to say - *Practice Note: Purazi Chipfakacha* v *Chris* 1972 AAC (vii).

The defendant should then be called upon to admit or deny the facts alleged in the claim - rule 10(2)(c) - and the court must record his plea and any counterclaim he desires to make - rule 10(2)(d). The purpose of this procedure is to discover what are the issues between the parties and by putting the various facts relied on by the plaintiff and requiring the defendant either to admit or deny each of them in turn, the issues basically become evident - *Kanyuka Sixpence* v *Egista a/b John Hawker* 1967 AAC 37.

In terms of rule 10(3), either party may for a sufficient cause request a postponement or adjournment, which the court may grant. In this regard, it must be recognized that summonses are prepared by a relatively junior official and if at the trial new issues are raised or if old issues are raised in a different form and a party asks for a postponement to call witnesses on such issues, the court should consider the application. If the presiding officer is of the view that there will be no prejudice to the party applying for the postponement if the trial proceeds forthwith, he should refuse it and proceed with the trial. If, on the other hand, he thinks there will be prejudice, he should postpone the hearing to a suitable date, which should be made clear to both parties at the time - *Tambudzayi's* case *(supra); Nosenga and Kefasi* v *Musadane* 1954 SRN 436. If a witness whose evidence is prima facie relevant does not attend through no fault of the party calling him, for example, if he is ill and unable to attend, a postponement ought to be granted to enable him to give evidence - *Practice Note: Chief Namauzhe* v *Shumba* 1975 AAC (v).

A witness should be sworn according to the form of religion he professes, provided that any person entitled to affirm instead of being sworn may so affirm - rule 11(1). A note should be made that a witness has been sworn prior to the commencement of his evidence - *Practice Note: Enock Kumalo* v *Themba Dumeya Nkomo* 1973 AAC (viii). If any person does not understand the nature, or recognize the obligation of an oath, he may be permitted to give evidence unsworn, provided he is admonished to tell the truth - rule 11(2).

Calling of evidence

If the defendant denies the facts in the claim, the plaintiff shall first adduce the evidence upon which the claim is founded, and thereafter the defendant shall produce the evidence in support of his plea - rule 12. If the onus of proof is on the plaintiff, then it is his duty to adduce evidence first - *Sandi Chikomba Chikungwuna* v *Wunganai Chiutsi* 1975 AAC 22.

Evidence of the outcome of the proceedings before a chief's court cannot be admitted in the district commissioner's court, since it amounts to no more than information that on whatever facts were put before the chief, he came to the conclusion he did - *Practice Note: Chari* v *Mathew* 1970 AAC (vi). Such information is quite irrelevant to the matter before the district commissioner's court. If, however, the chief's court was a court of competent jurisdiction, constituted by warrant in terms of the African Law and Tribal Courts Act *(Chapter 237)*, the defendant may properly plead *res judicata*, that is to say, that the matter has already been decided by a court of competent jurisdiction. A similar position arises when a matter decided in a district commissioner's court is then commenced afresh before a chief's court - *Mutandwa* v *Broko* 1957 SRN 516. Such a plea is not available if the chief's court is not such a court of competent jurisdiction - *Practice Note: Dzingirai Murefu* v *Rombesai Musori* 1971 AAC (v). Neither can a plea of *res judicata* be taken on the ground that the subject-matter of the trial has already been subject to an arbitration award - *Mangwiro* v *Matema* 1941 SRN 147. In order for such a plea to operate as a valid defence, it must be taken in the court of first instance and cannot be taken for the first time on appeal - *Kachingwe* v *Sitima* 1932 SRN 49.

The presiding officer may not advise the defendant what evidence should be brought in support of his plea at the close of the plaintiff's case - *Chanakira* v *Sande* 1951 SRN 268. Neither is the court permitted to call any witnesses without the consent of the parties, subject to the single exception that it may do so when it has to decide the best interest of a child, the custody of which it is called upon to determine - *Practice Note: Mazorodze* v *Chikombe Simon* 1973 AAC (vi). This exception is limited to the calling of witnesses whose evidence is likely to be material, such as the mother of a child whose custody is in dispute, where it is desirable in the interests of the child to subject the father's evidence to any available check and to receive any available evidence that might throw light on the character and qualification of the parents - *Practice Note: Grace Matumo* v *Charles Chabata* 1966 AAC (ix).

In any other circumstances it is an irregularity for a presiding officer to call any witnesses, as in doing so he may depart from his judicial detachment and travel beyond his judicial function, and while it is perfectly proper for a presiding officer to give some guidance to an unrepresented litigant in the presentation of his case, such guidance cannot be extended to calling for additional witnesses whom the parties themselves have not produced. If, after having heard the witnesses produced by the parties the presiding officer considers that the evidence adduced does not justify a final judgment, the only proper course to adopt is to grant absolution from the instance, although it is permissible in some circumstances to intimate that if further evidence becomes available the plaintiff could reinstitute proceedings. It is the responsibility of the litigants not the court to ensure that adequate evidence is adduced - *Practice Note: Mashonganyika* v *Taurayi* 1966 AAC (viii); *Raphael Moyo* v *Mugwagwa Moyo* 1977 AAC 5.

Notwithstanding any agreement of the parties, if the matter is commenced by one judicial officer and then adjourned and continued before another, the case must be heard *de novo* - *Hlambelo* v *Dandane* 1964 AAC 45. A record of evidence made by another presiding officer must necessarily be an insecure foundation on which to rest a decision of disputed questions of fact - *Practice Note: Tamayi Moyo* v *Maqude Kabo* 1966 AAC (xi), and a failure to adopt the proper procedure is enough to invalidate the proceedings - *Practice Note: Daniel Mbaira* v *Britto Maswi* 1970 AAC (xi).

A presiding officer has a clear duty to recuse himself in circumstances where he has, prior to the case, in his capacity as a district commissioner or district officer, given advice to one of the parties - *Practice Note: Mary Munjoma* v *Ferris Munjoma* 1970 AAC (ix).

Cross-examination

Each party, together with his witnesses are liable to cross-examination by the opposite party, and to re-examination. At the conclusion of evidence-in-chief and of cross-examination, the presiding officer is obliged to inquire whether the relevant party wishes to cross-examine or re-examine the witness, as the case may be - rule 13(1)(2).

If a party declines to cross-examine his opponent or his witnesses, a note should be made on the record, showing in addition that he was afforded the opportunity to do so if he had wished - *Matsike* v *Gwama* 1963 CAR 41. It is an irregularity to fail to invite a party to cross-examine - *Practice Note: T Chigwida* v *F Mazengera* 1962 SRN (vi).

Before a party may cross-examine his own witness as being hostile, it must appear to the court that the witness bears an inimical demeanour or an adverse attitude to the party calling him. The mere fact that the witness has given adverse answers does not necessarily make him hostile, and it is immaterial that the witness has on a previous occasion made an inconsistent statement - *Murambiwa* v *Chief Nyashanu* 1962 SRN 29. The refusal of a witness to answer questions put to him constitutes a contempt of court - *Practice Note: Chari* v *Mathew* 1970 AAC (v).

The court has the right to question witnesses and may at its own instance receive the evidence of any person whom the presiding officer believes is likely to give material evidence and who is within the precincts of the court and wishes to give evidence - rule 13(3).

If the evidence is scanty or ambiguous, the presiding officer should take it upon himself to question witnesses in some detail, so as to get a clear picture on the record of what each party alleges - *Paradza Chibova* v *Tatayi Museve* 1964 AAC 4. It is of importance, and the duty of the presiding officer to put such questions to witnesses as he thinks might assist to proper determination of the issues before him, particularly if the parties are not sufficiently competent to query in any useful manner matters raised against them, such as, for example, medical evidence of a technical nature - *Peter Ntenetzi* v *Timothy Mapango* 1965 AAC 36. In general the court should give every assistance possible to litigants who are not legally represented - *Kechemu* v *Marisa* 1953 SRN 371; *Mahomedi* v *Maganga* 1944 SRN 33, and in such circumstances a failure to cross-examine may be due to a complete ignorance of the purpose and function of cross-examination, rather than an admission of the other party's evidence - *Reuben Mhlanga* v *Mabula Masuku* 1967 AAC 9.

Examination of witnesses by interrogatories

Rule 14 provides for the examination of witnesses by interrogatories if the witness resides in a district other than that of the court, in any particular case, and prescribes the procedure therefor. However, recourse to taking evidence by this means should be resorted to only where it is clearly impossible for the witness to attend the trial in person - *Taruwinga* v *Mrewa* 1941 SRN 154.

Address

On completion of the evidence, each party or his advocate or attorney may in turn address the court in support of his case - rule 15. As a matter of practice the judicial officer should in every case invite each party to address him and if the right to do so is declined he should make a note to that effect on the record. Addresses can assist the court and prejudice may result if there is a failure to do so - *Practice Note: Elina* v *Julias* 1963 CAR (ix).

Parties in default

If at the time fixed for the hearing the plaintiff is in default the action may be dismissed with costs, but may be reopened on payment by the plaintiff of the costs awarded against him and on tender of a fresh claim form - rule 16.

If the defendant is in default, the court may proceed to hear the case and give judgment thereon. Provided that where the claim is for custody or divorce a rule nisi must be issued calling on the defendant to appear at a specified date and time, failing which judgment may be given in his absence - rule 17(1)(2). Before proceeding in terms of subrule (1), the judicial officer must satisfy himself that the defendant had had due and sufficient notice to attend - *Practice Note: Munyaradzi* v *Nyunga* 1975 AAC (vi); *Newton Chimedza* v *Murindagomo* 1977 AAC 17.

The court may require the plaintiff to give security for full restitution, before execution, and the defendant may at any time within two months from the date of judgment request that the proceedings be reopened. If the court is satisfied as to the excuse of the defendant for his failure to appear on the day of the hearing, and the defendant provides sufficient security, it must reopen the proceedings - rule 17(1).

The dismissal of a case in default of the plaintiff's appearance does not bar the reinstitution thereof on the ground that the matter is *res judicata* - *John Jack* v *Mojapelo* 1965 AAC 15.

Assessment of damages

A plaintiff must take all reasonable steps to mitigate his loss and a defendant is not liable for damages due to the plaintiff's failure in this regard - *Mandinyanya Kengere* v *Musoko Muchineripi* 1969 AAC 40. Moreover, if the quantum of damages has been agreed between the parties then there can be no variation of that agreement by one party in the absence of consent on the part of the other - *Tapera Chikunga* v *Muhambi Jack* 1964 AAC 70.

The court is not justified in refusing to award damages merely because the quantum of damages is difficult to assess. If it is clear that damage has been sustained and the best evidence as to the amount of that damage has been placed before the court, then the court must do its best, on the evidence before it, to assess the amount of damages to which the plaintiff is entitled. In doing so, in the absence of other evidence, the plaintiff's own estimate of the value of his loss may be acceptable - *Chikuwanyanga* v *Mupariwa* 1969 AAC 83.

(3) JUDGMENT AND APPEAL

Judgment

All judgments must be delivered in open court - rule 20(1). If neither party is in default it is not competent for the action to be dismissed. Either there must be judgment for the plaintiff, if he has established his case, or, if not, judgment for the defendant or absolution from the instance. Judgment for the defendant is appropriate where the defendant has established his defence, and where he has not absolution from the instance - rule 20(2); *Practice Note: Mary Jenje* v *Ben Kunaka* 1964 AAC (vii). Absolution from the instance cannot be granted in respect of an issue in which the onus is on the defendant - *Practice Note: Jane Maruta* v *Esther Katama* 1969 AAC (x); *Practice Note: Tafirenyika* v *Esther* 1965 AAC (vii).

It is important that when judgment is given in court, what is said is said after consideration and with due thought, in the knowledge that the parties are vitally interested in hearing what the presiding officer has to say about the case and his reasons for finding for one party and against the other. The interests of justice require that there should be no laxity on the part of the presiding officer in choosing his words or expressing his views or findings. It is most desirable if not essential, for the court to state in court whose evidence it finds acceptable, whose evidence it rejects and the reasons for its decision. It is far less preferable for such matters to be mentioned for the first time when reasons for judgment are given in writing - *Practice Note: Dabiya* v *Tichareva* 1963 CAR (viii). As a general rule of practice the court should give its impression of the witnesses, the way in which they gave their evidence and what reasons there are for accepting or, on the other hand, rejecting such evidence - *Practice Note: Clarkson Nkomo* v *Jonathan Jabangwe* 1965 AAC (vii). It is lawful for the court to find on any issue of fact, and to give judgment in respect of such finding on the evidence of a single, competent and credible witness. Where, however, there are two conflicting stories and the court, after searching for confirmation of one or other of the versions is unable to satisfy itself that the claim or defence, as the case may be, has been proved, then the presiding officer should order absolution from the instance - *Mary and Dayiri Tom* v *Musekiwa E Gwena* 1965 AAC 41.

Judgment may not be given for more than is claimed in the summons - *Marwhe and Rumane* v *Kwangwa Charlie* 1957 SRN 512; *Denere* v *Andinowangu* 1934 SRN 62, and must be formulated in terms of lawful tender, that is to say, in terms of dollars and cents. A judgment in terms of cattle can be made only when specific cattle are made the subject of the judgment - *Mbonisi Moyo* v *Tendayi Moyo* 1976 AAC 1. It is always open to the parties, once judgment has been delivered in terms of legal tender, to translate it into terms of cattle but such a translation cannot be recognised by the courts - *Baliwe Rabson* v *Nasu Obert* 1972 AAC 25; *Practice Note: Roseman Dlamini* v *Kariot Mtambo* 1971 AAC (vi).

The court may correct patent errors in its judgment or rescind or vary it if it was void *ab initio* or was obtained by fraud or mistake on the part of any party - rule 20(3). If after provisional judgment has been entered, the defendant wishes to contend that the judgment was procured by fraudulent evidence, the proper course is for him to sue for an order setting aside the judgment on that ground. It is not competent for him at that stage to appeal against judgment - *Changara* v *Office* 1966 AAC 18.

The powers to rescind or vary a judgment are subject to the provisions of rules 16 and 17, and may be exercised only after notice by the applicant to the other party or, if no application is made, after notice to both parties - rule 20(4).

Reasons for judgment

The purpose of giving reasons for judgment is so that a court of appeal, assessing the judgment in the light of the evidence and the argument addressed to it on appeal, will be in a position to determine whether or not the judgment is correct - *Practice Note: Mukayira* v *Manuel* 1966 AAC (vii); *Practice Note: Newarayi* v *Mukandah* 1963 CAR (ix). So that, when giving his reasons for judgment, a judicial officer should state his views on the credibility of witnesses, judging not only from their demeanour but from all the circumstances of their appearance in the witness-box, and when he has reason to doubt a witness he should give his reasons, and if he believes a witness he should equally give his reasons - *Practice Note: Mukayira* v *Manuel* 1966 AAC (vii). For example, if a witness made a bad impression because he was hesitant or evasive or over-voluble, then that reason for the impression should be stated and if possible, reference should be made to specific instances of hesitancy, evasiveness and so on - *Practice Note: Mots Kunaka* v *Phineas Chitengu* 1969 AAC (v).

Costs

Jurisdiction to award costs is conferred by sub-section (3) of section 5 of the African Affairs Act (*Chapter 228)*, which provides that the court of a district commissioner may in its discretion make an order as to costs. The power to make such an order as the court deems fit in this regard is contained in rule 27.

It is essential to the proper functioning of the courts that the conduct of litigation should be kept as simple, informal, and inexpensive as possible. The magistrate's court scale is no longer appropriate as a basis for assessing costs and the High Court scale is clearly too high. The proper approach for district commissioners to adopt is to quantify the costs by ascertaining the actual amounts disbursed in the process of instigating or defending the suit, and add any other reasonable amount, such as travelling expenses. Such a practice has the advantage that costs are kept more in proportion to the sum in dispute and the means of the parties than they would be under an existing statutory scale. In addition it obviates the necessity of taxation of a party and party bill. If, however, a district commissioner does order that a party and party bill shall be payable on the magistrates' court scale, he may not delegate the task of taxation according to that scale to the clerk of the court. So far as attorney and client costs are concerned, no scale is provided by statute for such costs and it follows that either the litigant and his lawyer have to specifically agree on the sum to be charged or there must be agreement *quantum meruit*. The former method is by far the more preferable - *Russell Samuriwo* v *Robson Dhlamini* 1975 AAC 9.

Where a plaintiff has a right to bring an action in the district commissioner's court, he should not be penalized in costs for exercising that right or for obtaining proper legal representation - *Pemha* v *Joshua Patrick Zuichemo* 1972 AAC 9. The court has no discretion to refuse to award the costs of legal representation simply because the case is shown to be a simple one - *Matilda Matangaidze* v *Peter Matangaidze* 1972 AAC 4; *Samuel Shumba* v *Johnson* 1973 AAC 3. Any party has the right to legal representation in district commissioners' courts (*vide* rule 8(1)), and in cases which raise difficulty, it is desirable that the parties should be represented, even though the damages ultimately awarded consist of a relatively small sum - *Julius Makondora* v *Togarepi Nyapadi* 1967 AAC 13.

There is no justification for depriving a party of costs simply because the damages claimed exceed those awarded - *Chanakira* v *Daka* 1966 AAC 20. On the other hand, if a party is to blame for unnecessary costs incurred through his failure to object to the jurisdiction of the court at the outset then he is liable for those costs - *Mandaza* v *Tawuya Stores (Pvt) Ltd* 1963 CAR 11. Moreover, where there is a defence which cannot be trusted and the plaintiff's case is also untrustworthy, the court should mark its disapproval of the defendant by making no order as to costs, even though he succeeds in defending the claim - *Zakiya & two others* v *Tavarwisa & Pomerayi* 1971 AAC 11.

Appeal procedure

Any person against whom any final judgment has been given may appeal against such judgment to the Court of Appeal but must note appeal within thirty days of such judgment, submitting his grounds of appeal and the nature of the relief sought - rule 26(1). The rule refers to a final judgment, but a default judgment is not a final judgment because a defendant has his remedy in the lower court. He can apply to reopen the proceedings in terms of rule 17 instead of appealing. However, once the time for reopening the proceedings has passed and the defendant is debarred therefrom, the default judgment does tak take on the nature of a final judgment - *Charumbira* v *Mariyekanda* 1977 AAC 20; *Newton Chimedza* v *Murindagamo* 1977 AAC 17. In calculating the period in which an appeal may be noted, the day on which judgment was given is excluded from the computation - *Kenneth* v *Enock* 1963 CAR 3.

A defendant is estopped from appealing against his own plea - *Dennis* v *Mhlungwa* 1952 SRN 309; *Youngs Mlalazi* v *John* 1969 AAC 14 - and it is not possible to appeal against a judgment to which the appellant has consented. He is bound by his consent unless it was invalidly obtained, in which case his remedy is not to appeal but to institute a fresh action in the same court for an order setting aside the judgment obtained by his consent, on the ground that that consent was invalidly obtained - *Potiphar Munkodya* v *Chinganga David* 1971 AAC 2.

While it is desirable that the parties should be notified at the conclusion of the trial of their right to appeal, there is no obligation to do so - *Ex parte Kachiwawa* 1958 SRN 545; *Practice Note: M L Muzata* v *Mahuraiswa* 1966 AAC (vii). However, when an appeal is noted the clerk of court must inform the appellant of the steps he must take for prosecuting the appeal, and the court may allow or delay the execution of judgment - rule 26(3). In doing so, it may require deposit of such property as is adequate security for the satisfaction of the judgment of the Court of Appeal - rule 26(4). Any appeal not prosecuted within three months from the date of noting shall be deemed to have been abandoned - rule 26(2). When an appeal is noted, the district commissioner must inform the respondent - rule 26(5).

B. PROCEDURE IN THE COURT OF APPEAL

General

Sessions of the court are held, and the time and venue for sessions for the hearing of appeals are subject to the direction of the President thereof - rule 3 of the Court of Appeal Rules. The court *should determine appeals with the minimum of formality and it should not rely on any technicalities to prevent it from resolving what are the real issues between the parties* - per Beadle ACJ in *Tambudzayi* v *Samuriwo* 1976 (1) RLR 27 (AD) at 29.

Every appeal is instituted in the form of a notice of appeal signed by the appellant or his legal representative and noted within thirty days of judgment. The notice is delivered to the clerk of court who transmits it, with the original and three copies of the record, to the registrar. At the same time, the appellant must serve one copy of the record on the respondent - rule 4(1).

The notice of appeal must set forth concisely and under distinct heads the grounds of objection to the judgment appealed against and the exact nature of the relief sought - rule 4(2). Notwithstanding this rule, however, the court will hear an appeal even where no grounds of appeal have been stated - *Mangwiro* v *Matema* 1941 SRN 147 - or both parties are in default - *Mangwiza* v *Mwarume* 1929 SRN 25. However, new claims may not be raised on appeal - *Nzira and Chitimbe* v *Zwinavashe* 1947 SRN 161; *Pisira* v *Enoki Sonokele* 1954 SRN 446 - although a new point may be taken if the court is of the view that the appellant was not solely to blame for its omission in the court below - *Sitayi* v *Lomacala and Mhlahla* 1930 SRN 33. This indulgence is not extended to a woman who fails to object at the trial that the person who assisted her at the trial as her guardian is not her true guardian, and she is estopped from appealing in her own name and taking the point for the first time on appeal - *Puce* v *Sandalamu* 1943 SRN 14.

Appeals out of time

The registrar is precluded from accepting any notice of appeal that is out of time unless leave to appeal out of time is sought and any application for an extension of time should be filed with the registrar - rule 5(2)(3).

Application for an extension of time in which to note appeal is made in court, stating the reasons upon which the application is based. A copy of the application and supporting affidavits are served on the respondent - rule 6(2). The applicant must show something which entitles him to ask for the indulgence of the court - *Chiramba* v *Elinah* 1964 AAC 67. The respondent may file a reply with supporting affidavits within seven days of the application being served on him - rule 6(3). A failure to adhere to this practice may result in prejudice to the respondent - *Majoni* v *Tawurayi* 1969 AAC 16.

A failure to advise a party of his right to appeal is not of itself a ground for condoning the late noting of appeal *Ex parte Kachiwawa* 1958 SRN 545 - although this does not preclude an applicant from putting this ground forward as an excuse, nor that he might say similarly that he did not understand his right of appeal. But an application for condonation should be supported by affidavits from the applicant and his witnesses, in proof of any fact relied upon by him, and any explanation that he does put forward should be supported by evidence of its genuineness - *Practice Note: Ex parte Maponga* 1958 SRN 525.

The affidavits must contain as full and detailed an explanation as possible - *Lighton Madebgwe* v *Jamu* 1964 AAC 19 - and while no hard-and-fast rule can be laid down, they must show something which entitles the applicant to ask for the indulgence of the court - *Ex parte Kapita* 1958 SRN 608; *Ex parte Yotam* 1947 SRN 176 - and the decision on condonation of the delay will be governed by the merits of the reasons for the delay and not the merits of the main appeal - *Ex parte Usanga* 1955 SRN 485.

The court may grant or refuse the application (rule 6(3)(d)), and in making its decision, it will usually be guided by the degree of noncompliance, the explanation therefor, the importance of the case, the prospects of success on appeal, the respondent's interest in the finality of his judgment, the convenience of the court and the avoidance of unnecessary delay in the administration of justice - *Lovemore Mapaura* v *Erica* 1970 AAC 1; *Elliot Ncube* v *Pesulani Phiri* 1969 AAC 9.

Consequently, condonation may be refused if it is shown that the applicant knew of his right to appeal but could not be bothered to find out the time in which to do so - *Ex parte Tsikayi* 1959 SRN 619 - or if on a consideration of the evidence there is no reasonable prospect of success on appeal - *Ex parte Bebura* 1959 SRN 627; *Martin Chaponda and Saize* v *Piki* 1964 AAC 9; *Ignatio Maposa* v *Gertrud Mkomozana* 1975 AAC 14; *Petros Sithole* v *Moses Rukunda* 1976 AAC 6. Neither is a short delay necessarily a sufficient excuse - *Nyamadzawo* v *Priska* 1938 SRN 25. Moreover, a party is bound by the acts or omissions of his attorney, and the attorney's negligence is not a sufficient excuse for condonation of the delay - *Lighton Madebgwe* v *Jamu* 1964 AAC 19; *Ex parte Mutizwa* 1958 SRN 527 - although the failure of the attorney to pay the appeal fee, provided the appeal itself was noted timeously may be - *Ex parte Patsika* 1954 SRN 435; *Ex parte Tafirenyika* 1954 SRN 454.

Equally, a delay occasioned by faulty legal advice may be sufficient excuse - *Ex parte Jona* 1954 SRN 419; *Petros Sithole* v *Moses Rukunda* 1976 AAC 6 - or that a refusal to grant the application may result in a miscarriage of justice - *Practice Note: Jojina* v *Dembetembe* 1963 CAR (vii). Where the custody of children is in issue, and the welfare of the child paramount, an application for condonation will normally be granted - *Magret and Mangure* v *Johannes* 1963 CAR 24; *Mbonisa Moyo* v *Tendayi Moyo* 1976 AAC 1.

After evidence has been heard to determine the application, it is competent for the court to proceed forthwith with the hearing of the appeal, provided the parties are agreeable - rule 6(3)(c).

Presence of the parties and abandonment

Either of the parties may intimate to the registrar, either directly or through the clerk of court, that he do not wish to be present or legally represented at the hearing of the appeal - rule 7. In which case notice of set-down need not be served upon him - *Practice Note: Venancio Musiyiwa Muzenda* v *Timothy T Mtengwe* 1972 AAC (vi).

Similarly, an appellant may at any time before the hearing abandon his appeal by giving written notice to the registrar. In this event the appeal is deemed to have been dismissed with costs - rule 8. The court has no power to dispense with the payment of the appeal fee, prescribed in rule 26 of the District Commissioners' Court Rules (Appendix I) - *Makore* v *Chikowore* 1966 AAC 115. The fee forms part of the costs for the prosecution of an appeal - *Norido* v *Hlawu Jamela* 1970 AAC 16 - and when an appeal is withdrawn, application for the refund thereof must be made timeously - *Isaac* v *Kamoto* 1953 SRN 319. On the withdrawal of an appeal, costs may still be incurred if, due to short notice or notice not being received in time by the respondent, the respondent is put to unnecessary expenditure, for example having to travel long distances - *Cosmos* v *Makoni* 1970 AAC 18. A judgment of the trial court cannot be abandoned. If the respondent seeks to do so, the court may allow the appeal, even if noted out of time - *Enock Godfrey* v *Nediyo* 1961 SRN 21.

Set-down

The registrar, on the instructions of the President, causes notice of set-down to be served on the appellant and respondent - rule 9(1).

It is important that as a matter of routine a *domicilium citandi* is obtained from each party at the conclusion of the trial, before the parties leave the courtroom - *Practice Note; Mazero* v *Farashishiko* 1964 AAC (viii). The purpose thereof is to facilitate service, but if the appellant fails to notify the court he has moved it will not necessarily mean that the appeal is not properly before the court, even though the appellant is unaware that it is being heard - *Practice Note: Percy and Emily Mukumbe* v *Maria* 1969 AAC (x); (*contra: Practice Note: James Ndava* v *Harry Chakanyuka* 1968 AAC (v).

Hearing and adjournment

The court will not interfere with a judgment on the sole ground that it is not strictly within the pleadings - *Ginza* v *Johannes* 1936 SRN 92. Neither will it disturb the trial court's finding of fact when the weight of evidence is not clearly against it - *Aaron* v *Mbosha* 1938 SRN 19; *Magukwa* v *Chobono* 1938 SRN 31; *Munyengetergwa* v *Katapa* 1938 SRN 43; *Tinapi* v *Chiwenga* 1938 SRN 45; *Matiringana and Kwaramba* v *Usayi* 1940 SRN 104; *Mabetshu* v *Menyezwa* 1944 SRN 25.

The court will interfere with an award of damages only in cases where the award was made on a wrong principle or because, in the opinion of the court, they are so unreasonable as to be out of all proportion to the injury sustained - *Makore* v *Hlupe Ignatius* 1964 AAC 51. This latter criterion applies to an original award of low damages as it does to high damages, but a court of appeal does not readily interfere with the award of damages, the assessment of which is primarily the responsibility of the trial court. The mere fact that if a court of appeal had been sitting as a court of first instance it would have awarded greater or lesser damages does not necessarily justify a different assessment from that made by the trial court. It follows that a court of appeal will not interfere unless there is some striking disparity between its own estimate of damages and that of the trial court, and, further, unless there is some unusual degree of certainty in its mind that the estimate of the trial court is wrong - *Julius Makondora* v *Togarepi Nyapadi* 1967 AAC 13.

If it appears to the court proper, it may adjourn an appeal or application for such period as it thinks fit - rule 10. Similarly, the court has the power to direct the proceedings to be reopened for the taking of evidence - rule 11. But, before doing so, the appellant must show that his application does not offend against established principle and that proper notice of the application has been given to the other party - *Lameck Marovagondo* v *Dipa Garise* 1975 AAC 38.

When remittal to hear further evidence is asked for by a party who has failed, despite having the opportunity to do so, to produce such evidence on a point plainly in issue, the application should normally be refused, unless the court is of the opinion that such a course is in the interests of justice - *Zakaria Rusere* v *Tambureyi Newman* 1969 AAC 18. Similarly, if it appears to the court that a plaintiff would be unable to adduce additional evidence in support of his claim were the matter to be remitted, it will not normally grant the application but will order absolution from the instance - *Practice Note: Nyamande* v *Majura Chiura* 1966 AAC (xii).

The proper procedure to adopt when a matter is remitted for investigation is to put the relevant questions to the party concerned and then allow the other party to cross-examine on those points - *Practice Note: Emily Nkono* v *Esther Nkala* 1967 AAC (vii).

Costs

The jurisdiction to award costs is conferred by subsection (7) of section 5 of the African Affairs Act (*Chapter 228*), which provides that the Court of Appeal may in its discretion make an order as to costs. In terms of rule 12, any costs awarded may be taxed by the registrar, subject to review by the President. The established practice of ordering a party to pay the costs of his opponent in appropriate cases should not be disturbed - *Samuel Shumba* v *Johnson* 1973 AAC 3. The court also has the power to reconsider an award of costs made in the lower court - *Chanakira* v *Daka* 1966 AAC 20.

A litigant appearing on his own behalf as appellant or respondent may be awarded his costs, and such costs may include his travelling and subsistence expenses - *Gideon Pepukai* v *Mzanywa* 1966 AAC 16.

Appeal to the Appellate Division

Notice of appeal from the court to the Appellate Division is lodged with the registrar within twenty-one days from the date of the court's decision - rule 14 - but the President may allow an extension of this time, as he may allow an extension of any time prescribed in the Rules - rule 15.

C. EVIDENCE

General

The degree of proof required in any civil case, including adultery cases, is by a preponderance of probabilities - *Kefasi* v *John* 1958 SRN 612 - and the onus is on the plaintiff to establish his case - *Practice Note: Simon Ndhlovu* v *Edward* 1973 AAC (viii). The preponderance of probabilities may be found in the probabilities arising from the evidence and all the circumstances of the case - *Practice Note: Samuel Ntuli* v *Simon Mlambo* 1970 AAC (xii).

It is highly undesirable in a district commissioner's court for evidence to be put in by consent, as it is probable that the parties do not appreciate what constitutes permissible evidence and what is or should be admissible - *Practice Note: Chinyai* v *Norris* 1963 CAR (vii).

A medical report must be produced by the medical officer who made it, and it is irregular to admit it by consent - *Meri* v *Merita* 1966 AAC 53 - and a record of a criminal case must be produced through the officer in whose custody the record is - *Aaron Jaravasi* v *Tembekire* 1959 SRN 662. Such criminal records are generally inadmissible as being irrelevant but a previous plea of guilty may constitute an admission which may be proved in subsequent proceedings - *William Join* v *Regina Chiyaka a/b Chinyama* 1967 AAC 24; *Ben Mhandu Tsodzo* v *Simon Chideme* 1977 AAC 22 - and it may be permissible to consider as evidence the record of a previous case, provided the consent of the parties is obtained - *Tigere and Hana* v *Dick Chokumarara* 1963 CAR 35; see also *Fanyana* v *Nyika Magwisi* 1969 AAC 63; *Peter Ntenetzi* v *Timothy Mapango* 1965 AAC 26.

There is no need for a confession to be corroborated and all that is necessary is for the court to be satisfied that it was freely made and not under any sort of compulsion or threats. A confession which is otherwise inadmissible is not rendered admissible by the presence of corroboration - *Monica* v *Jenje Muchenje and Mbewu Tapambwa* 1963 CAR 5. A confession by a defendant, particularly in a seduction case, is very important evidence and the circumstances in which it was made should be investigated with great thoroughness. Consequently, the court should take upon itself the task of probing the alleged confession as fully as possible - *Practice Note: Augustine Mupfuni* v *Aaron Jacha* 1973 AAC (v).

Opinion evidence by non-experts is inadmissible for the reasons that, firstly, such evidence cannot materially assist the court in arriving at a decision and, secondly, if non-experts could testify, each party would probably produce as many witnesses as possible to provide evidence supporting his case, and the investigation would thus become absurd - *Practice Note: Augustine* v *Godwin* 1976 AAC (ii).

Sufficiency of evidence

It has been held that corroboration in cases of adultery is no longer required, as being inconsistent with customary law - *Samuel Shumba* v *Johnson* 1973 AAC 3. Nevertheless, it is submitted that in cases where reliance is to be placed solely on the confession of the woman more than ordinary care is required - *Paul Masembur* v *Juawo Yawo* 1972 AAC 28 - and in certain circumstances some corroboration of the woman's confession may be desirable for the just determination of the case.

Corroboration is evidence of what took place at the time the event leading to the action occurred: it may be that of an eyewitness or it may be evidence of incidents that happened prior to the event or afterwards. It must be independent testimony which affects the defendant by connecting or tending to connect him with the actionable event. It must, in some degree, be consistent with the story told by the plaintiff and inconsistent with that of the defendant - *Ruka* v *Pfidze* 1963 CAR 47. For example, the confession of a woman, in an action for adultery, may be corroborated by an extra-curial admission by the defendant to a third party - *Jona* v *Muchonisi Ernest* 1954 SRN 461.

Although in an action for seduction, corroborative evidence is not usually required - *Paul Masembura* v *Juawo Yawo* 1972 AAC 28 - where the defendant in his plea denies the seduction then, depending on the circumstances of a particular case, some corroboration may be necessary, even if the defendant does not call or give any evidence in support of his denial - *George Maswimbo* v *Stanley* 1965 AAC 5. The failure of the defendant to give evidence cannot be construed as corroboration - *Practice Note: Ruben Zimbura* v *Josiah* 1966 AAC (xiv).

An action for seduction is decided on a balance of probabilities and the process of balancing the probabilities takes place after all the evidence has been led. If the balance is against the plaintiff she loses the case. If it is in her favour, she wins. Where corroboration is sought, evidence of opportunity does not amount to such corroboration - *Gamanya* v *Saida Kakora* 1958 SRN 587.

It is most desirable that in seduction cases the girl gives evidence herself, if she is available as a witness - *Kadoho* v *Lawrence Chitsomba* 1970 AAC 23. However, in customary law it is possible for a father to bring an action for damages for the seduction of his daughter without calling his daughter as a witness. If such a course is adopted, it is necessary that the court scrutinizes the father's claim closely and should be wary of accepting that a seduction has occurred unless there is clear proof to that effect. Such proof might be afforded by a confrontation between the plaintiff and his witnesses, and the defendant, where the purpose of the confrontation is to ascertain if he had had sexual intercourse with the girl, and during the course of which the defendant confesses to such intercourse - *Tobias Madondoro* v *Dapi Chirwa* 1970 AAC 19.

The evidence of an emissary (*munyai*) of money paid by the defendant as an admission of liability may sufficiently corroborate the evidence of the woman - *Robert* v *Mugwagwa* 1954 SRN 458 - but the evidence of a midwife as to what a mother said at the time of birth, while it may be admissible in tribal courts, is not admissible in a district commissioner's court if it is said in the absence of the other party - *Gratiano Nyangowa* v *Manenje Ndondo* 1965 AAC 25. A mother is estopped from denying the defendant's paternity of her child where he has paid damages for seduction and *rutsambo* - *Hlale* v *Dziyakwi* 1938 SRN 34; *Puce* v *Sandalamu* 1943 SRN 14.

In an action for adultery, it is essential to prove the existence of a registered marriage either by customa or Christian rites - *Tiki Parima Makuni* v *Nyandoro Jairo* 1970 AAC 22. In the absence of registration, the husband has no right to claim damages for adultery, but an action may be brought by the father or guardian of the woman for seduction - *Shumba* v *Tichareva* 1958 SRN 547. Moreover, it is necessary for the plaintiff to prove that the defendant knew that the woman was married - *Bwanari Dick* v *Simon* 1969 AAC 1. This is so even where the wife has become a prostitute - *Mudoni* v *Felix Tutani* 1955 SRN 491, and if he cannot do so and the woman has held herself out as a prostitute to the defendant the husband will not be able to recover damages for adultery - *Samanyika Mwale* v *Mangwiro* 1955 SRN 493. If the plaintiff and his wife were married by Christian rites the same burden of proof prevails but the common law must be applied in deciding the liability of the defendant - *Honye* v *Wakayi* 1955 SRN 496.

It must follow from what is said above that the defendant may successfully resist an action for damages for adultery if he can show that he was not aware of the woman's married status and that she held herself out as a prostitute. He is entitled to infer the latter if the woman accepts money from him - *Tawonezwi* v *Taziwinga* 1957 SRN 518; *Shoniwa* v *Jenje* 1958 SRN 543. It was held, in *Lenard Andina* v *Wamututu* 1954 SRN 433 that where the undisputed evidence disclosed that a woman received money for two acts of sexual intercourse and stayed away from her home with different men for various periods and in a drunken state had intercourse with several men in a lavatory and had other lovers, the court could properly conclude that she was a prostitute.

In actions for divorce it is necessary to prove the existence of a valid marriage - *Tawonerera* v *Matenzeyi and Muchabayiwa* 1953 SRN 359; *Manyanga* v *Matipadza and Boniface Tederere* 1953 SRN 401. And, even if both parties agree to a divorce, evidence must be led to establish recognized grounds - *Etrudi and Mutadzi* v *Chimondo* 1960 SRN 671 - and just cause - *Naomi and Chiresi* v *Magara* 1953 SRN 331. It is not competent to grant a divorce on the bare consent of the husband, even though in customary law this formality is not required - *Magara's* case *(supra)*.

In disputes as to the amount of *lobolo* paid or agreed upon in respect of a marriage, the entry in the marriage certificate is the best evidence - *Gideon* v *Butete and Butete* 1949 SRN 201 - and where both parties to an action were present at the registration they are estopped from contesting the sum entered in the marriage certificate - *Tabiya and Sineki* v *Nyama* 1963 CAR 15. If this evidence does not exist then the evidence of the *munyai* should be preferred, unless there is good reason for disbelieving him - *Chipazura* v *Tigere* 1941 SRN 130; *Willie* v *Mapfumo* 1950 SRN 244.

Presumptions

It is now an established rule that no irrebuttable presumption of adultery arises when it is proved that the woman concerned has struck her alleged adulterer with her *shashiko*, that is to say, the front apron of skin. In any event, the act has no significance at all unless it is done spontaneously with the traditional *shashiko* and no presumption arises at all if the striking is done with an undergarment which implies that the outer apparel is still worn, for there has not been that complete disregard for modesty when, spurred by indignation at being rejected by her lover, a woman was prepared to expose her more intimate self by removing her only front garment for the purpose of striking him with it - *Marimo* v *Tasarirenamo* 1957 SRN 510. However, where a man and a woman sleep in her hut in the absence of her husband, the presumption that adultery took place is so strong that it requires the clearest evidence to rebut it - *Shoniwa* v *Jameson* 1950 SRN 238 - and a similar presumption will arise in actions for seduction, where the evidence shows that the girl spent the night with the defendant in his hut - *Sigumila* v *Ben Sibanda* 1964 AAC 48.

It is presumed that an unmarried woman is a virgin, and he who alleges to the contrary must prove it - *Stanley Machakanja* v *Martin* 1963 CAR 19.

If the man admits intercourse, although denying paternity, the woman is to be believed on the paternity issue even if it is proved that other men have been intimate with her, unless the circumstances disclose that it was physically impossible for the man to be the father of the child or unless the court is of the opinion that the woman is unworthy of belief - *Martin's* case *(supra)*. Moreover, when a man marries a woman after having lived with her prior to the formal marriage and after paying damages for seduction, as well as *rutsambo*, it is presumed that he is the father of any child born after the marriage. In such a case, both the woman and her father are estopped from later denying the husband's paternity - *Hlale* v *Dziyakwi* 1938 SRN 34. So that evidence of illegitimacy is inadmissible in an action for the custody of a child born *stante matrimonio* *Maratu* v *Mbangetwa* 1941 SRN 157. Similarly, a child conceived during the subsistence of a marriage but born after its dissolution is presumed to be a child of the marriage, and strong evidence is required to rebut this presumption - *Ndoro* v *Mapfumo* 1942 SRN 166.

A presumption of legitimacy is applied to a child of an unregistered customary marriage in which the main elements of marriage are present - *Zimunu* v *Chakawarika* 1933 SRN 60.

Evidence in the Court of Appeal

The Court of Appeal has power to direct that in any case on appeal the proceedings shall be reopened for the taking of any evidence or in relation to any other matter and any evidence or other matter so directed by the court may be taken or dealt with either before the court itself or before any district commissioner's court - rule 11.

As a matter of practice, new evidence will be heard in the Court of Appeal only in exceptional circumstances *Madziwa* v *Chirenda* 1939 SRN 63; *Mandizwidza* v *Tiribanu* 1939 SRN 67 - and additional evidence will be adduced only where there appears to have been a miscarriage of justice - *Tolongo* v *Mbasela* 1944 SRN 41.

The Court of Appeal has no review jurisdiction, so that if a party wishes to complain that the judicial officer wrongly refused to admit evidence, and the record of the trial does not disclose what was the evidence sought to be adduced by the party (evidence upon which he relies in the prosecution of the appeal) the court must disregard it. In such circumstances the correct procedure is to institute review proceedings in the General Division of the High Court - *Practice Note: Mercy Chopamba* v *Obadiah Chopamba* 1971 AAC (vi); *Magwegwe* v *Christopher Guni* 1973 AAC (ix).

CHAPTER III

FAMILY LAW

A. MARRIAGE AND DIVORCE

Section 1. *Lobolo*

Section 2. *Civil Marriage*

Section 3. *Customary Marriage*

B. WOMEN

C. CHILDREN

Section 1. *Children of a Christian Marriage*

Section 2. *Children of a Customary Marriage*

Section 3. *Illegitimate Children*

A. MARRIAGE AND DIVORCE

(1) LOBOLO

General

The valuable consideration given by the husband for the privilege of marrying his wife is known as *lobolo* and is one of the recognized elements in bringing about a recognized union. Besides being a kind of marriage settlement, it is calculated to add dignity and respect to the woman; it adds to her value to her husband, and is likely to ensure for her kind and considerate treatment - *R* v *Guteyi & others* 1915 SR 49. It is one of the fundamental features of an African marriage - *Chote* v *Matiye* 1974 (1) RLR 302 (AD) - and there can be no valid marriage until the terms of *lobolo* have been agreed upon between the husband and the woman's guardian - *Godwin Mudzimu* v *Kenneth Gomwe* 1975 AAC 16; *John Paradzayi* v *Nyiwe Dzirutwe* 1964 AAC 73. Ownership of *lobolo* passes on marriage - *Mbidzeni and Diki* v *Siya* 1938 SRN 21.

Role of the Munyai

The *munyai* is the representative of the suitor's father and he negotiates with the woman's father. However, a son should not function as the *munyai* for his own father - *Madziwa* v *Chirenda* 1939 SRN 63 - for, *semble*, if a *munyai* is related to either of the parties or has an interest in the outcome of later proceedings, the weight which may be attached to his evidence will be lessened. Whereas, generally speaking, in the absence of documentary evidence, the evidence of the *munyai* should prevail on such questions as the amount of *lobolo* agreed upon - *Chipazura* v *Tigere* 1941 SRN 130 - and to whom it was paid - *Tasarirobona Mrindi* v *Turi* 1967 AAC 28 - unless there are strong reasons for disbelieving it. See also *Sevi and Ginatsio* v *Roberts* 1958 SRN 562.

Assessment of the amount

Where an amount has been paid by the suitor to the woman's father at the time of the marriage, in connection with the marriage, the court ought to attempt to ascertain how much is payment of *rutsambo* and what was part-payment of *lobolo* - *Elliot Mhlanga* v *Grace and Weston Mundicha* 1970 AAC 33. In doing so, if cattle have formed the calculation of the amount paid and there are children of the union, then in determining the correct amount of cattle, it is possible to say that one head of cattle is a correct assessment for each child, although this cannot constitute a hard-and-fast rule - *Amon Nyakunhuwa* v *Elijah Hove* 1970 AAC 36.

Payment

There can be no valid customary marriage until the terms of *lobolo* have been agreed upon by the husband and the woman's guardian - *Godwin Mudzimu* v *Kenneth Gomwe* 1975 AAC 16. Generally speaking, it is contrary to custom for *lobolo* to be paid to anyone except the woman's guardian - *Sambo* v *Moyo and Makumalo* 1939 SRN 58 - but in *Amoni* v *Marika and Chikanda* 1954 SRN 422 it was held that it was not unusual amongst non-indigenous Africans in urban areas for the mother of the girl to accept payment of *lobolo* and give consent to her daughter's marriage. The provision of cattle for the payment of *lobolo* by the head of a family for his direct descendant constitutes an irrevocable payment of *lobolo* - *Magwisi* v *Kombayi* 1947 SRN 177. Payment of damages for seduction does not form part of the payment of *lobolo* in respect of the subsequent marriage - *Nyengerayi* v *Sandaram* 1949 SRN 205.

Very often the question of payment is the only matter left outstanding before solemnization and if the court were to order specific performance in pursuance of the agreement to pay *lobolo* this might well encourage the parties to regard the matter as finalized and so to refrain from taking steps to have the marriage solemnized. It is clearly the policy of the African Marriages Act *(Chapter 238)* to regularize customary marriages by solemnization and registration. To allow the parties to form the belief that an order for specific performance for payment of *lobolo* finalized the question, in the circumstances outlined, could well defeat the policy of the Legislature - *Choto* v *Matiye* 1974 (1) RLR 302 (AD). Consequently, the failure of the husband to pay the agreed *lobolo* is a practice to be discouraged - *Nendaya and Tigere* v *Zidenga* 1955 SRN 499. This may be done by awarding custody of the children to the mother pending payment of the outstanding *lobolo* - *Nzira and Chitimbi* v *Zwinavashe* 1947 SRN 161 - unless it would not be in the best interests of the children to do so, for example, due to the moral behaviour of the mother - *Dayimano* v *Kgaribaitse* 1931 SR 134.

Where an intended marriage is broken off after part of the *lobolo* has been paid, an amount which is fair and reasonable in the circumstances may be recovered by the husband, even if it was he who broke off the negotiations - *Isaiah Muwori* v *Petros Sabau* 1967 AAC 25; *(contra: Sangirayi* v *Zimgowa* 1938 SRN 37*)*.

If an uncle provides *lobolo* for the marriage of his nephew, he is in the same position as a father providing for his son, and there is an obligation on the nephew to behave as a son would - *Dodo* v *Makawuya* 1934 SRN 75 - and on the death of the nephew, so long as the widow remains with the heirs, the uncle has no claim for the return of the cattle he provided - *Chirimanyemba* v *Msau* 1928 SRN 1.

Rights arising from payment

As a general rule, if *lobolo* has been paid, the custody of the children of the union are awarded to the husband on dissolution of the marriage - *Ida and Ben* v *Chombe* 1947 SRN 151. However, the children must be his own, for a man cannot pay *lobolo* for a woman which will give him a right to her unborn child of which he is not the natural father - *Mungazi* v *Chibanda* 1937 SRN 1.

Following a divorce where the wife is awarded custody of a female child, the husband may in certain circumstances be entitled to *lobolo* accruing from the marriage of that child - *Mucheno* v *Chisamba and Chisamba* 1940 SRN 87 - but this does not apply where the child is an adulterine child and the husband takes no steps to secure damages for the adultery and where, in any event, *lobolo* paid in respect of the marriage has been returned to him with increase - *Jakata* v *Kwanayi* 1941 SRN 137.

Return of lobolo

The following factors are relevant in claims for the return of *lobolo*: (1) the fault for the breakdown of the marriage - *Daniel* v *Teresa* 1972 AAC 17; (2) the service of the woman; (3) the existence at the time of divorce of some counter-claim, usually involving the children of the marriage or maintenance of the wife by her family - *Mateko* v *Matikare* 1963 CAR 57; (4) the refusal of the husband to attempt reconciliatio and (5) prejudice to the wife's chances of remarrying by reason of the husband's delay in suing for divorce - *Simon* v *Puweyi and Takaidza* 1964 AAC 1.

If the husband accepts in full the return of *lobolo* then he cannot claim custody of any children - *Harry* v *Nomi and Esinati* 1947 SRN 160.

When *lobolo* is returned than a cash value may be placed on the cattle paid, but the value must be assessed as at the date of the trial, not at the time of original delivery of the cattle - *Simon's* case *(supra)*.

It is the date of the marriage on which the ownership of cattle passes and this is not in all circumstances the date of registration of the marriage; no increase in cattle occurring after the date of the marriage can be claimed as returnable - *Mbidzeni* v *Diki and Siya* 1938 SRN 21. The court should closely scrutinize a claim for the return of any increase - *Nyamadzawo* v *Mandaza* 1930 SRN 38 - and should not accept an unproved assumption thereof - *Masiyiwa* v *Mchanetsa and Kasinawuyo* 1938 SRN 27.

No customary marriage can be considered legally dissolved until at least a portion of the *lobolo* paid has been returned by the wife's family - *Muchabayiwa* v *Emelia and Kumire* 1957 SRN 520. (In Ndebele custom the father of a wife who dies or is barren must either provide another wife in her place or, alternatively, return at least a portion of the *lobolo* - *Sigonqo* v *Matombi and Pameti* 1958 SRN 585.)

Lobolo is returnable on a proportionate basis, regard being had to the number of children born of the marriage - *Mchenje* v *Kunaka* 1912 SR 207. No settled scale can be laid down and the return of a proportion of the *lobolo* must depend on the circumstances of each case - *Siyamakayi* v *Tawodzera* 1934 SR 68. However, when assessing the proportion which ought to be returned, the following factors may be taken into account:

(a) The number of children of the marriage, the duration of the marriage and the good behaviour of the wife - *Mbidzeni and Diki* v *Siya* 1938 SRN 21.

(In the districts of Mtoko, Mrewa, Darwin, Marandellas, Lomagundi, Urungwe and Hartley, it was held, in 1947, that *lobolo* is returnable on the death of a wife, less a proportion for the children of the marriage living at the time of the wife's death and the period the wife lived with her husband - *Jarata* v *Furutsa* 1947 SRN 157.) A substantial reduction was made when, although the break-up of the marriage was due to continual quarrels, the wife had carried out her marital duties for many years, had borne six children and was old and past the child-bearing age - *Kaduku* v *Msodzi and Mshori* 1939 SRN 56. Conversely a wife's barrenness may entitle the husband to a refund of a major portion of the *lobolo* - *Teresa and Gwabanai* v *Akupusa* 1958 SRN 549 - although a deduction can be made for the wife's services during the subsistence of the marriage - *Japondo* v *Elisa and Jack* 1945 SRN 73.

(b) The defendant's adultery - *Kamingipa* v *Jengera and Murapi* 1940 SRN 92.

(c) The plaintiff's adultery - *Tandiwa* v *Muchaneta and Chingombe* 1965 AAC 59.

(d) Repudiation of the wife without just cause - *Nyakudja* v *Nsodzi and Mshori* 1939 SRN 70; *Shingirayi* v *Chiwoneso* 1953 SRN 342.

(e) Gross illtreatment of the wife by the husband - *Mucheno* v *Chisamba and Chisamba* 1940 SRN 87; *Moses* v *Nubula and Charlton* 1944 SRN 38; *Chada* v *Paurai* 1948 SRN 189; *Kathleen Siwira* v *Amoni* 1953 SRN 365.

(f) The wife's repeated desertion and adultery - *Muchaneta and Kanje* v *Timbe* 1953 SRN 395.

(g) Adulterous pregnancy - *Chitaguta* v *Esta and Masiyambiri* 1944 SRN 31.

Although a grown-up family of four or five children will normally preclude the repayment of *lobolo* in full, a portion may be returnable if most of the children died before attaining their majority - *Mkwesa* v *Maponga* 1946 SRN 106. As a general rule, customary law permits the deduction of only one head of cattle in respect of each child of the marriage - *Ngonya and Gasa* v

Nyamayendga 1945 SRN 70 - another for the wife's services - *Chamunorgwa* v *Dzokera and Sungayi* 1946 SRN 101 - but this rule is not invariable and each case must depend upon its own circumstances, including the question of which party was responsible for the break-up of the marriage - *Dudzai* v *Mapanda* 1943 SRN 20; *Tinavapi Machinjike* v *Bunhu Mujikwa* 1969 AAC 78 (in which cases two head of cattle for each child was considered a reasonable deduction).

Where a loan is made to the father of a girl not of marriageable age, on the understanding that it will be repaid to the lender as part of *lobolo* for the girl when she attains marriageable age, the transaction will be regarded as one of pledging, in contravention of subsection (1) of section 11 of the African Marriages Act (*Chapter 238*) and the court should not entertain a claim by either party - *Chapotoka* v *Mugombi* 1941 SRN 134. To grant relief in such circumstances is *contra bonos mores* - *Shonai* v *Nyamfarira* 1941 SRN 132. Any claim for the return of the sum advanced on the grounds that the girl will not consent to the union is also unenforcable, for the same reasons - *Ndabambi* v *Raisi* 1937 SRN 9. Where *lobolo* has been agreed but not paid, it may be claimed by the wife's guardian after dissolution of the marriage, provided that the husband will be allowed to deduct a portion by way of reclaim in the ordinary way - *Job Kekana* v *Josiah Jakachira* 1967 AAC 31.

Subsidiary payments

The payment of *rutsambo* is not an essential of marriage but it is evidence of acceptance by the payee as a suitor for the hand of the girl - *Kulumo* v *Diyana & others* 1944 SRN 35. Where such payment consists of a large sum, however, it is really a part of the marriage consideration and should be treated as forming part of the *lobolo* - *Kufakwedu* v *Mandizwidza* 1936 SRN 85. This aspect apart, however, *rutsambo* is not returnable once the marriage has been consummated and the parties have lived together - *Zwomazva* v *Josephine* 1973 AAC 22 - provided that *(a)* there has been offspring of the marriage, *(b)* the amount of the payment is within traditional limits of one beast or its local value, and *(c)* the woman has not unlawfully deserted her husband in the very early stages of the marriage - *Jambawu Madondo* v *Mudzamiri* 1973 AAC 24.

The *chipanda* system is based on the principle that cattle received in connection with the marriage of a daughter should be used to provide a wife for her brother, and a particular brother and sister may be linked for this purpose. Where, however, a man has received one *chipanda* he has no claim as of right to more than that one, merely on the ground that *lobolo* from a sister of full blood must automatically belong to him as *chipanda* - *Gariwa* v *Chigwedere Musarurgwa* 1958 SRN 533.

Chisaba is a customary payment by the son-in-law when the girl is a virgin on marriage, but it cannot be claimed if the girl has prior to the marriage lost her virginity, although it may be claimed from her seducer - *Mashako Pombi* v *Stephen Chimombe* 1953 SRN 412. It is not a payment that can be recovered as part of the return of *lobolo* on the dissolution of the marriage - *Chikanya* v *Chigwada* 1929 SRN 21.

When there is no marriage, the girl's guardian is not entitled to a beast *ngombe yo amai* for damages in a seduction claim. For the handing over of this beast is an essential incident of marriage - *Tambi* v *Sailos* 1953 SRN 346. Neither is it returnable as part of the *lobolo* returned on dissolution of the marriage - *Kuzowomunhu* v *Eneleta and George* 1949 SRN 199.

Kubvindira or *rubvunso* is only returnable on the failure of marriage negotiations, and only then if such failure is attributable to the girl. It is not returnable on the failure of the marriage - *Maredza* v *Lamuel Chiduza* 1965 AAC 49. But for a detailed consideration of the subsidiary payments that may be returned, see *Elias Murove* v *Edward Bernard Chakawizira* 1975 AAC 33, where the Court of Appeal accepted the expert evidence of Chief Seki as correctly setting out the customary law applicable in the circumstances of that case.

(2) CIVIL MARRIAGE

Preparation

Africans who wish to marry by Christian rites must be allowed to wait until they are qualified to do so if they so elect - *Sangirayi* v *Zimgowa* 1938 SRN 37.

Legal Consequences

Where Africans have elected to marry by Christian rites, then all the consequences of a Christian marriage must follow, including the principles governing its dissolution - *Flora Sebetso* v *Maxwell Sebetso Rathuso* 1946 SR 119. And this is so even if the marriage by Christian rites follows upon or is in addition to a customary marriage - *Mucheno* v *Chisamba* 1940 SRN 87. So that custom can exist side by side with a civil marriage only when it does not violate the principles of the latter - *Dayimano* v *Kgaribaitse* 1931 SR 134.

Divorce - general

Applying the principle that in cases where the parties have been married by Christian rites the common law must apply and the relevant formalities followed, then in cases of divorce the fact of the marriage must be proved by the production of a marriage certificate - *Gideon* v *Butete and Butete* 1949 SRN 201 - or a certified copy thereof - *Practice Note: Rison* v *Jeremiah* 1958 SRN 526.

Moreover, such a marriage can be dissolved only on the grounds permitted by the law governing marriage according to Christian rites, for it would be repugnant to natural justice, where an African has contracted a civil marriage, to apply customary law inconsistent with such civil marriage - *Ellen* v *Jim* 1931 SR 118. Consequently, where the plaintiff caused his wife's desertion by his own adultery, it was held that he had no ground of action for divorce founded on malicious desertion - *Leah* v *Joshua* 1932 SRN 39. The plaintiff must allege and prove a ground of divorce valid in common law; 'incompatibility of temperament' is not such a ground - *Beatrice and Njambwa* v *James* 1944 SRN 46. Neither is it competent to restore conjugal rights to each other. Such an order can be made only against the party who is to blame for the desertion - *Practice Note: Tondhlana and Dhliwayo* v *Tondhlana* 1964 AAC (viii). If cruelty is the ground of divorce, then it must be shown that the defendant's conduct was such as to make the continuance of married life insupportable - *Angeline Chiutsu* v *Dennies Garisa* 1969 AAC 70.

Notwithstanding the application of common law to civil marriages, if the plaintiff is the wife and she has been sent to her home by the defendant then she can sue only if assisted by her guardian - *Chinyeruse* v *Jessina* 1953 SRN 333.

Divorce - specific grounds

When an African commits adultery with a woman who is married by Christian rites, the principles of common law, not those of customary law, prevail - *Katina* v *Mutandiwa* 1966 AAC 7. Consequently, since *dolus* is an essential ingredient of liability for adultery, damages are not recoverable against a defendant who at the time sexual intercourse took place was ignorant of the fact that the woman was married. It is therefore a good defence for the defendant to show that he bona fide and on reasonable grounds believed the woman to be unmarried - *Thomas* v *Josiah* 1959 SRN 655. Similarly, although in customary law a claim for damages for adultery lies against a man who has intercourse with a woman after the death of her husband but before the *kurova guva* ceremony has been conducted, this right of action does not exist where the marriage was by Christian rites - *Mukarakate Chidakwa* v *Chitaukiri* 1963 CAR 90.

If, in an action for divorce on the grounds of adultery the defendant is in default, the court should grant a final order upon the facts proved and not issue a rule nisi - *Gladys and Matembele* v *Jonathan Mangwiro* 1963 CAR 1.

Where the ground of divorce is that of malicious desertion, the claim should be one for restitution of conjugal rights, failing which divorce, and there should be proof that the desertion was malicious - *Munetsi* v *Sarudzani a/b Miwirimi* 1942 SRN 169. It is therefore not competent to dispense with a restitution order and grant a final order of divorce outright, because the issue of a restitution order is based on a fixed principle of public policy and is not something which the guilty party can abandon. Consequently, an order for the restitution of conjugal rights is essential unless the court is able, on a consideration of the applicability of the provisions of subsections (3) and (4) of section 2 of the Matrimonial Causes Act *(Chapter 39)* to grant a final order for divorce - *Flora Sebetso* v *Maxwell Sebetso Rathuso* 1946 SR 119.

(3) CUSTOMARY MARRIAGE

Essentials

The essential requirements of a customary marriage are threefold; (1) the consent of the woman, the woman's guardian and the man, (2) the agreement as to the amount of *lobolo*, and (3) a formal handing over of the woman by the guardian - *Abigail Kurangwa a/b Kurangwa* v *Elijah Chanakira* 1966 AAC 29 - although this last requirement may be dispensed with where the parties have lived together for a number of years and consider themselves man and wife - *Dumase and Sailos Chekani* v *Adamu* 1958 SRN 594.

So far as the consent of the woman is concerned, this is an essential prerequisite - *R* v *Majoni* 1963 R&N 143 (SR), and such consent must be at the stage when the marriage is about to be completed - no reliance can be placed on a previous consent, when the girl was not of marriageable age - *R* v *Chokumarara* 1945 SR 88. Before solemnization of a marriage, marriage officers must satisfy themselves that the woman freely and voluntarily consents to it - *R* v *Mutumba* 1958 R&N 391 (S

A marriage officer must, moreover, satisfy himself on the other essential requirements contained in sub-section (1) of section 7 of the African Marriages Act *(Chapter 238)* including the consent of the husband to the marriage. Although the latter may not strictly form a part of customary law, it would be contrary to natural justice and morality for a man to enter into a marriage with a woman he is not prepared to accept as his wife - *Abigail Kurangwa's* case *(supra)*.

An action for breach of promise to marry is unknown in customary law. However, such an action would not be repugnant to natural justice and morality, so Roman-Dutch law cannot be invoked to give such a cause of action - *Erikanos Mupasiri* v *Maggie a/b Mufandaedza* 1968 AAC 5.

Domicile - effect of

Where a member of one tribe elects to live with and among members of a different tribal group, issues arising between himself and members of that tribal group are decided according to the customary law obtaining in the tribal group amongst whom he has settled and not by that of his origins - *Sigonqo* v *Matombi and Pameti* 1958 SRN 585. Conversely, where the parties are both members of a foreign tribe then, it seems, the custom of that tribe prevails and will, for example, govern the essentials necessary for the completion of a customary marriage, although not the question of the custody of a child of the marriage. That question and other consequences of the marriage, should be settled in accordance with the law of the country where the marriage was entered into - *Leya and John Phiri* v *Masauso Banda* 1958 SRN 605; *Ishmael Ngwira* v *Mavies and Thomas Zimba* 1964 AAC 22; *Rhodia* v *Mandala* 1942 SRN 179; *Reya and Kapita* v *Zuze* 1951 SRN 269. Neither can the customs of foreign or immigrant Africans in conflict with the law override the law of the country - *R* v *Ngono et Uxor* 1915 SR 1.

Where a man from Rhodesia marries a foreign woman and the marriage is solemnized in Rhodesia then the customary law of this country will apply to the consequences of marriage - *Kapeta and Mairesi* v *Mugwagwa* 1954 SRN 464. On the other hand, where a man domiciled abroad marries a Rhodesian woman, she takes her husband's domicile and must be prepared to return with him to his country of origin - *Thom* v *Raina and Ben* 1952 SRN 294.

Donations between spouses

Presents of cash, clothing or food to the wife before or after marriage by the husband are not recoverable - *Mako* v *Chivadza and Kunatsa* 1945 SRN 79. Similarly, gifts to a woman with whom a man had lived for a period of three years were held not recoverable - *Wilson Mataga* v *Eriza and Mutandwa* 1953 SRN 391.

Divorce - general

Certain formalities must take place between the parties and their families in an endeavour to surmount the difficulties that have arisen before an action is instituted for divorce, and before such an action can succeed it must be shown that such endeavours have been made - *Lucia and Chakanyuka* v *Gandidzanwa* 1953 SRN 388 Once family matters are the subject of litigation, however, it is desirable for the court to settle all possible sources of dispute between the parties - *Practice Note: Philimon Mpofu* v *Solomon and Edith* 1969 AAC (vii).

In view of the provisions of subsection (3) of section 3 of the African Marriages Act *(Chapter 238)* a court has no jurisdiction to hear a divorce action in relation to an unregistered marriage because no marriag between the parties is recognized. However, a claim for the return of *lobolo* may be heard - *Joseph Tinga* v *Joshua Shekede* 1970 AAC 30. Neither has a district commissioner's court any equitable jurisdiction to dissolve a marriage; it can do so only on the establishment of a recognized ground for divorce - *Tapfumaneyi Alexander* v *Tandiwe Musayeya* 1973 AAC 17.

In an action for divorce, unless the custody of children or the return of *lobolo* is specifically claimed or counter-claimed the court should not make any order with respect to these matters and both custod and *lobolo* in such circumstances may be the subject of a separate and subsequent action. If, however, the question of custody has been fully investigated and no hardship or prejudice will be suffered by either party, an order may be made in respect of such custody - *Bowen Sibanda* v *Aidah Mpofu and Jacob Hanyana* 1964 AAC 44; *Dolika and Kalamizu* v *Musadane* 1954 SRN 420.

Divorce - specific grounds

Impotence of the husband constitutes a valid ground for divorce - *Sheriwa* v *Risi and Mubayiwa* 1944 SRN 27 - as it would be contrary to natural justice and morality to refuse such relief to the wife - *Chawa* v *Bvuta* 1928 SR 28. At Shona law, divorce is not the only remedy for the impotence of the husband. For the husband may send his wife to cohabit with a male relative, for the purpose of conceiving a child. They must agree to this course, however, and the husband must give a token to the relative concerned. Failure to make proper arrangements may render the relative concerned liable in damages for seduction - *Mondiwo* v *Muwirimi* 1952 SRN 296.

Incompatibility is not a ground for divorce - *Mchemwa* v *Chandengerwa* 1954 SRN 428 - but physical cruelty, such as would make the continuance of married life dangerous to one of the spouses is - *Munemo* v *Mandiyera and Sengeza* 1943 SRN 12. So are repeated assaults on the wife - *Sheriwa's* case *(supra)*; *Jokonya* v *Diana and Machingura* 1944 SRN 44 - but discontent caused by a quarrel is insufficient - *Jennifer Moya* v *Mavunga Gande* 1971 AAC 21. Corroboration of acts of cruelty is not normally required - *Freddie Mavunga* v *Anna Murape* 1970 AAC 27 - and it is not competent for a court to issue a restitution order when this ground of divorce is relied upon - *Practice Note: Eveline Gumbo* v *Langton Muyambo* 1969 AAC (v).

When the ground of divorce is malicious desertion, a restitution order is appropriate only when the marriage is by civil and not by customary rites - *Practice Note: Gahadzikwa* v *Ednah* 1965 AAC (viii); *Practice Note: Christopher Bzwifu* v *Chipo a/b Mica Zisengwe* 1969 AAC (xi); *semble*, a wife is entitled to a divorce on the ground of her husband's prolonged desertion - *Jokonya* v *Diana and Machingura* 1944 SRN 44 - and where a woman made unsuccessful attempts to effect a reconciliation it was held, in the circumstances, she had adequately proved that she had been rejected by her husband, and was entitled to an outright order of divorce - *Tasiyana* v *Meriya* 1969 AAC 76. Conversely, provided that the defendant does not oppose the action, a plaintiff who has committed adultery and driven the defendant wife away from the matrimonial home may himself be granted a divorce on the ground of desertion - *Mugwagwa* v *Nyadzisu and Tigere* 1940 SRN 106.

Damages for adultery are recoverable on two separate and distinct grounds; on the ground of injury or *contumelia* inflicted upon the husband and, secondly, on the ground of the loss of the comfort, society and service of the wife. The estimate of damages on the first ground may vary very greatly. For example, substantial damages may be awarded if out of his affection for her the husband is prepared to forgive his wife's lapse and condone her misconduct, but nevertheless proceeds against her seducer. Conversely, if a man is married to a prostitute it is difficult to see a court awarding him any damages - *Saida* v *David* 1965 AAC 38. It follows that where the husband has condoned his wife's misconduct with the defendant on a previous occasion but the defendant and the wife persisted in the same misbehaviour, indicating clearly it was not a case of sudden temptation, this may be a reason to increase the amount of the damages - *David* v *Phillimon* 1967 AAC 1.

When a man and a married woman sleep in her hut in the absence of her husband, the presumption that adultery took place is so strong that it requires the clearest evidence to rebut it - *Shoniwa* v *Jamesen* 1950 SRN 238. However, in other circumstances, the degree of proof by circumstantial evidence which is required is that degree which will lead to the reasonable inference that adultery did take place - not merely that it might have done - *Dune* v *Nyamuru* 1945 SRN 66. In the case of a denial, the admission of a woman to her co-wife that she has committed adultery, without corroboration, is insufficient evidence of the adultery - *Idi* v *Mabaza* 1946 SRN 143. A claim merely for interfering with a woman in circumstances in which the maxim *volenti not fit injuria* can be said to apply cannot succeed among the Vazezuru - *Lawrence* v *Musomali* 1951 SRN 259.

The fact of a wife's adultery lowers her value - *Kamangira* v *Jengera and Murapi* 1940 SRN 92 - and the proper person to bring an action therefor is the woman's husband, rather than her brother or natural guardian -

Mahomedi v *Maganga* 1944 SRN 33 - even though he may have condoned the adultery - *Hega Kenani* v *Phillimon Chifamba* 1963 CAR 44. But if the marriage has not been registered in terms of the African Marriages Act (*Chapter 238*) then no cause of action for adultery exists - *Samuel* v *Chimugaruwe* 1969 AAC 4; *Maso* v *Nyamuya Zhuwankinyu* 1971 AAC 1 - although her guardian has *locus standi* to claim damages for seduction - *Mureza and Anna* v *Ziyai* 1958 SRN 590; *Magwaro* v *Taurayi* 1966 AAC 25. In the case of actions for adultery brought by unsophisticated litigants in person, the court should ask pertinent questions, in order properly to determine the case - *Practice Note: Magolis Mukogo* v *Ganganisa* 1970 AAC (xi). The onus is on the plaintiff to prove that adultery occurred, but when a husband and wife, by acting in concert, have arranged matters in advance so that the defendant commits adultery with the plaintiff's wife and the husband then sues for damages, the defendant can successfully resist the claim by proving the collusion between the plaintiff and his wife. Clearly, the onus of proving such collusion rests with the defendant - *Jema* v *David Manhare* 1973 AAC 1.

Moreover, where a husband delays the issue of a summons and continues to live with his wife, who has another child by him, he may be held to have condoned the adultery and is thus barred from divorcing his wife - *Nyasha Raphael* v *Emily* 1976 AAC 47.

It is accepted that absence of knowledge of a woman's status is not a valid defence in customary law on which a man could rely for escaping the consequences of irregular intercourse with her, in the shape of a claim for damages for adultery brought by her husband if she is a married woman - *Nyaumba* v *Murapa* 1975 (2) RLR 138 (AD) (followed in *Maria & another* v *Murimbika* 1976 (1) RLR 385 (AD)). To this principle of customary law there are exceptions, for example, in urban areas where it is not always possible or easy to ascertain whether a woman is married or not - *Fibion Zinyemba* v *Freddy Baya* 1966 AAC 40. Thus, where a woman went alone to a beerhall in an urban area, denied she was married and behaved in an immoral way, it was held in the subsequent action for adultery that the claim for damages should fail - *Enock* v *Davide* 1959 SRN 657. But the onus of proving that a woman is a prostitute is always on the defendant - *Tobias Gudidu* v *Kenneth Mapungani* 1965 AAC 12. It should not be thought, however, that simply to show that a woman received payment for her services is sufficient to prove her a prostitute. For it is no defence that a woman entered into an illegal contract to receive money from the defendant - *Chikaisa* v *Amos* 1962 SRN 15 - whether or not intercourse actually occurred - *Useni* v *Zhuwakinu* 1953 SRN 386.

Maintenance

In customary law, when a woman and her children are maintained by her father in the absence of her husband, her father has no claim against the husband for maintenance unless he has first sent them to the husband's father, and he refuses to maintain them - *Mado* v *Skudamedzi* 1942 SRN 193.

Section 9 of the Matrimonial Causes Act *(Chapter 39)* in so far as it provides for the making of orders for maintenance after divorce permits the making of such orders following dissolution of a customary marriage - *Simon Machongwe* v *Christine Farusa* 1972 AAC 21; *George Mazorodze* v *Jeneth* 1970 AAC 38 - as well as a marriage by civil rites - *Gomese* v *Agnes* 1973 AAC 20. However, in terms of section 10 of the Maintenance Act *(Chapter 35)* the court has a discretion to award or refuse to award maintenance to a spouse who has committed adultery, where such adultery has not been condoned - *Ignatio* v *Gertrud Nkomozana* 1973 AAC 15.

B. WOMEN

General

There is a presumption that a woman is incompetent to enter into a contract - *Elizabeth Makola* v *Gondongwe* 1953 SRN 407 - but this may be rebutted if the woman can be shown to be emancipated, for example, living in an urban area, earning her own living - *Practice Note: Exavier* v *Dolan* 1960 SRN 677. And a woman who gave her illegitimate child into the keeping of another, agreeing to pay a particular sum for its maintenance, was held to be bound by the agreement - *Rusiya a/b Samuel* v *Lucy a/b Banwell* 1954 SRN 455.

Moreover, a married woman may own property acquired by her own labours, which will not be subject to her husband's control - *Rabecca and Musiyima* v *Vurayayi* 1958 SRN 571 - including cattle - *Nyongwana* v *Mariye* 1947 SRN 182; *Chamurwa* v *Elizabeth Chakava* 1947 SRN 153 - and her pots and other utensils, although not necessarily those utensils bought by her husband for use in the house - *Mutizgwa* v *Helida and Tafira* 1958 SRN 565. Notwithstanding this position, where a woman claims cattle from another it must be shown in evidence that she has the right of ownership. Without such proof the court should award absolution from the instance - *Hlambase* v *Wana* 1937 SRN 4. Where the parties' way of life and the transactions between them are so far removed from the incidents and customary way of life of the African people that it would be contrary to the justice of a particular case to apply customary law to the solution of the property dispute between them, then common law may be applied - *Jirira* v *Jirira & another* 1976 (1) RLR (GD). Nevertheless, in general the customary law rule applies and a husband is entitled to his wife's wages. If, however, he allows her unrestricted use of them then he is deemed to have consented to such a course and is estopped from claiming a refund of them - *Pasco Nyamariwa Gunda (and Mr Mkushi)* v *Margaret Faina & Boniface Monyani* 1976 AAC 31.

Subject to the suitability of the individual concerned, in Ndebele custom a woman may be appointed as a guardian - *Mabigwa* v *Matibini* 1946 SRN 117.

Seduction

An action for seduction lies whether the woman seduced is a virgin or not - *Muza* v *Mbunjwa* 1943 SRN 17; *Shadreck Chitima* v *Gideon Danatu* 1962 SRN 27 - although the measure of damages will be affected by the moral behaviour of the woman *(infra)* - *Makiwa* v *Makina* 1943 SRN 1. The law does not allow a woman to sue for her own seduction - *Nira* v *Marete and Ngando* 1947 SRN 175 - and damages are claimable despite the rejection of the man by the woman -

Wiston Chikuwe v *Nyanzira* 1964 AAC 41. The claim is not one for sentimental damages, so the death of one of the parties does not terminate the action - *Nzuwa* v *Mark Makuwa* 1971 AAC 39.

A man who seduces a girl must pay damages for seduction before he tenders *lobolo* - *Nyengerayi* v *Sandaram* 1949 SRN 205 - and the damages do not form part of the *lobolo* - *Mosse Boniface* v *Johannes* 1961 SRN 9; *Gabriel Tayengwa* v *Tuburayi* 1976 AAC 11. The damages are known as *muripo* and are paid to the claimant. If the defendant also tenders *mereka*, to atone for the harm done, and, later on, *chiredzwa*, and these payments are accepted, he may acquire custody of the illegitimate child born of the seduction - *Kapisi* v *Magwayi* 1937 SRN 10 - although these payments also do not form part of the *lobolo* - *Nyengerayi's* case *(supra)* - and do not confer any right on the man to proceed to marriage - *Jubajuba* v *Hendrick* 1945 SRN 57.

Damages are awarded not only to compensate the girl's guardian for the diminution in the *lobolo* he can expect when the girl marries, but also for any other financial loss suffered by him through the wrongful act of the seducer - *Percy Budiyo* v *Peter Chimivedzi* 1974 AAC 13. In assessing such damages certain factors should be considered, viz:whether the girl was a virgin, whether pregnancy resulted, the character of the girl, the social standing of both parties, and whether intercourse was persisted in - *Aggrey Chingombe* v *Tonderi Mudzi* 1973 AAC 32; *Edward Ndhlovu* v *Dogo Malaba* 1959 SRN 639. In addition, the rising cost of living is a factor which should not be ignored - *Simon Moyo* v *Mawere Mapetere* 1974 AAC 11. Equally, in appropriate circumstances, exemplary damages may be awarded - *Fani Sibanda* v *Elijah* 1956 SRN 507 - and damages were increased where a breach of trust was a feature of the seduction - *James* v *Keyi* 1962 SRN 16 - and reduced when the court felt that a proper consideration was the humble social standing of the girl - *Eneas Hove* v *Marara* 1973 AAC 34; *Leonard Ruredzo* v *Mvelase* 1970 AAC 50. It is not proper, however, to attach a condition to an award of damages, that the sum paid as damages should be taken into account if the parties agree subsequently upon the amount of *lobolo* to be paid - *Practice Note:*

Manyore Ringi v *Bereredzo Bonda* 1970 AAC (x).

While it is doubtful if a claim for breach of promise to marry exists in customary law, an expressed desire to marry followed by a lack of interest in the girl may be regarded as an aggravating feature in assessing damages - *Gratiano Nyangowa* v *Manjenje Ndondo* 1965 AAC 25.

In Ndebele custom damages were not claimable in respect of a girl who was not a virgin. This custom has now fallen into disuse. However, an action for seduction should not, in Ndebele custom, be heard until after the birth of the child because damages are not payable unless the girl becomes pregnant - *Ngwabi* v *Malundu* 1951 SRN 275. This position may now, however, be in a state of uncertainty. In 1965, it was held, in the Nkai District, under Chief Madhliwa, that damages were claimable even if the girl was not made pregnant as a result of the seduction. Customary law is not static and the Ndebele customary law may have changed over the years. If so, then evidence of such changes should be heard - *Everest Dube* v *Chief Myinga* 1965 AAC 1. Nevertheless, in cases where there is a reasonable doubt and the defendant strongly denies seduction and paternity, the hearing should be postponed pending the birth of the child - *Ruke* v *Tose* 1946 SRN 82 - particularly if the defendant is likely to be prejudiced - *Chris Faranando* v *Loidi Karasa Nyuru* 1976 AAC 66 - and even though particulars in the pleadings properly indicate when and where the seduction took place - *Gratiano's* case *(supra)*.

This is not an immutable rule but it is based on the sound reasoning that sometimes the parties will arrange a marriage or other settlement of the case before birth, or further evidence may arise which can be of crucial importance in identifying the seducer. For example, there might be a marked resemblance between the child and the defendant. Additionally, the existence or otherwise of the child must affect very seriously the award of damages - *Bulawayo* v *Muchenje* 1976 AAC 18. The proper procedure is to obtain confirmation that the girl is pregnant at the commencement of the trial and then adjourn the case. No useful purpose is served in hearing the plaintiff's case prior to such adjournment - *Practice Note: Augustine* v *Godwin* 1976 AAC (ii).

In an action for seduction, no claim lies for the loss of earnings due to pregnancy - *Joel Susondo* v *Willie Rutsito* 1965 AAC 8 - for no such claim is known to customary law - *Mashako Pombe* v *Stephen Chimombe* 1953 SRN 412 - although this may form a part of the lying-in expenses - *Nyoni* v *Mamova* 1949 SRN 216 - and a claim may arise for maintenance following birth of the child - *Huchu* v *Magomo* 1966 AAC 6. Neither may a man set off the favours he has given the girl he seduced against the damages payable for the seduction - *Tabana* v *Gumani* 1962 SRN 23.

Where the undisputed evidence shows that a woman is a prostitute, no damages may be claimed for her seduction - *Lenard Andina* v *Wamututu* 1954 SRN 433 - and even if it is not shown that she is actually a prostitute, her previous behaviour with other men may be such that it would be morally wrong to allow an action for seduction to succeed - *Tokorekoria* v *Patrick Mtutu* 1953 SRN 384; *Gamanya* v *Saida Kakora* 1958 SRN 587.

If a payment of *rubvunso* has been accepted by the woman in acknowledgement of her suitor, and cohabitation follows, then no claim for seduction lies against the man - *Simon* v *Manukusa* 1946 SRN 132; *Chamunorgwa* v *Nyamayaro Timothy* 1958 SRN 602.

Even if there have been negotiations for marriage following seduction, but these have broken down, the girl's guardian is not entitled to receive a beast *ngombe yo amai* for the handing over of this beast is an essential incident of marriage and if there is no marriage it cannot be claimed as damages for seduction *Tambi* v *Sailos* 1953 SRN 345.

Widows

No female may inherit property in customary law, but where the State makes a gratuity payable to the dependants of a deceased estate, the widow is entitled to a share of it - *Juniah and Juniasi* v *Nawa* 1949 SRN 210. Moreover, a widow is entitled to maintenance at a reasonable rate proportionate to the value of such estate, pending its distribution - *Ganda* v *Chinamo* 1946 SRN 110, but not if the marriage was neither solemnized nor registered - *Ex parte Seti & others* 1963 R&N 681 (SR).

If a widow refuses to be inherited or there is no one to inherit her, and she returns to her own people, then a portion of the *lobolo* may be claimed - *Mjaka* v *Jerimani* 1946 SRN 127. However, if having refused to be inherited, she later remarries, the heir may claim the *lobolo* accruing therefrom - *Jamu* v *Jim and Takaziweyi* 1939 SRN 49.

C. CHILDREN

(I) CHILDREN OF A CHRISTIAN MARRIAGE

Custody

It is an established principle when a court dissolves a civil marriage that in awarding custody of any children of the marriage the moral and material welfare of the children shall be paramount. The only qualification to this principle is that unless the best interests of the children at customary law would be repugnant to natural justice and morality, then customary law should decide the issue - *Garadi* v *Annah* 1959 SRN 663. In deciding what are the best interests of the child, the court must obtain details of how the child would live with either parent, how it would be cared for, what arrangements there are for schooling, and all other aspects of the home environment - *Joshua* v *Martha* 1976 AAC 20.

Accordingly, if it is not in the best interests of the child to award custody to the mother, the court is quite justified in giving it to the father, irrespective of any law or custom to the contrary. If it appears that the mother is equally suitable as a guardian then such law or custom should be allowed to prevail if it is in her favour - *Dayimano* v

Kgarabaitse 1931 SR 134. But even if, contrary to customary law, the custody of a female child is awarded to the mother, the father is still entitled to any *lobolo* that may be paid for her on her subsequent marriage - *Gatsi* v *Dokasi* 1932 SRN 51.

Consequently, as in customary law the father is prima facie entitled to custody, even in a Christian marriage it is incorrect necessarily to regard the innocent party as prima facie entitled to custody - *Nguni* v *Sophia and Boniface* 1963 CAR 28. It should be remembered that the dissolution of a civil marriage and its consequences are governed by fixed principles of policy and justice, and the attributes of customary law only exist side by side with the civilized status in so far as they do not violate such principles - *Anafi Robert* v *Annie Isiah* 1964 AAC 55. Generally speaking, therefore, it will be in the best interests of the child if the mother is given custody until it reaches the age of seven and only thereafter should the father have custody according to customary law - *Gilbert Chinogara* v *Beaula Chinogara* 1970 AAC 43.

If the father of a child dies, the custody of his children is decided between the mother and their father's father, according to the moral and material welfare of the children. When the result of the application of such a test is indecisive then customary law should be applied and custody awarded to the grandfather - *Esnad Ndebele and Josiah* v *Togo Ndebele* 1965 AAC 23.

Adulterine children born to a woman during the subsistence of a marriage 'belong' to the husband - *Lydia* v *Masumbu* 1939 SRN 74 - and upon the marriage being dissolved the husband is entitled to the custody of such children, in the absence of anything to indicate that to award custody to him would be contrary to the moral and material welfare of the children - *Tabita and Jasi* v *Tawonezwi* 1961 SRN 33.

Guardianship

Provided that an award of guardianship, as opposed to custody, would not be contrary to customary law, such guardianship should be awarded to the father of a child - *Anafi Robert's* case*(supra)*. In the case of the death of the father, guardianship should be determined by customary law - *Tabitha Chiduku* v *Chidano* 1922 SR 55 - and, save in exceptional circumstances, should be awarded to the deceased father's father - *Esnad Ndebele's* case *(supra)*.

(2) CHILDREN OF A CUSTOMARY MARRIAGE

Custody

Where *lobolo* has been paid in a customary marriage, the custody of the children will be awarded to the husband unless there are very good reasons to the contrary - *Jockoniah* v *Simanga* 1967 AAC 34 - and this applies even if the marriage has not been registered - *Shoniwa Rackswell Chinamano* v *Mariyoti Gurajena* 1974 AAC 3; *Manuel* v *Kerina and Nono* 1964 AAC 7; *Practice Note: Ben* v *Juhana and Jowaki Antonio* 1958 SRN 523. The question of the moral and material welfare of the children arises if the other party questions the suitability of the father to have custody of the children - *Jack Museyemwa* v *Samson Mupandacharo* 1964 AAC 34. If this issue is raised then the court must have evidence before it entitling it to depart from the normal rule as to custody - *Arinesi and Shawati Nguwa* v *Elias* 1964 AAC 63 - and may call any witnesses it chooses irrespective of whether the parties agree or not - *Practice Note: Benjamin Mackenzie* v *Chambulangauda* 1971 AAC (v). In deciding the issue, it is the best interests of the child, and not the rights of any particular claimant, that are paramount - *Kufahakurotwe* v *Ajida* 1966 AAC 10. Thus, where the mother was a religious and competent social worker and the father a violent and habitual drunkard, the court awarded custody to the mother - *Mildred Mungofa* v *Julius Mungofa* 1971 AAC 24.

Provided the court satisfies itself that it is in the best interests of the children - *Tobias* v *Mandizwidza* 1968 AAC 7 - children of very tender years should not be removed from the custody of their mother -

Dumase and Sailos Chekani v *Adamu* 1958 SRN 594 - although before such an order is made, evidence should be heard that this is a course in the best interests of the children - *Nyakadzargwa* v *Lucky* 1961 SRN 26. In certain circumstances, custody may be awarded to a person who is not a parent - *Bope* v *Scotch* 1961 SRN 19. It has been accepted as a general principle that when a child reaches the age of seven years and it has been in the custody of the mother until that time, it is prima facie reasonable to remove it to the custody of its father. This, however, is not an immutable rule; it is merely a reasonable solution to the problem of which parent should have the custody where no other significant factor emerges as to what is the correct order to make - *Pemha* v *Joshua Patrick Zuichemo* 1972 AAC 9.

Bearing in mind that it is the child's best interests that are paramount, whether the father has paid *lobolo* in full will be a secondary, although relevant consideration - *Kufahakurotwe Simon* v *Ajida (2)* 1967 AAC 42 - although a father whose conduct is otherwise faultless may be deprived of custody until the payment of outstanding *lobolo* has been made - *Jeri* v *Saniso and Mutambiranwa* 1958 SRN 579; or may not be allowed to exercise his right of custody until payment of *lobolo* is complete - *Nzira and Chitimbi* v *Zwinavashe* 1947 SRN 161. He also loses custody when *lobolo* is returned to him - *Portoriro* v *Samson Burangwa* 1964 AAC 11. It must be remembered, however, that custody is an issue between the parents, whereas an adjustment of *lobolo* is an issue between the husband and the wife's guardian. Consequently, the traditional practice of linking an award of custody with an adjustment of *lobolo* is not competent, the best interests of the child being the paramount consideration - *Mbonisa Moyo* v *Tendayi Moyo* 1976 AAC 1. In view of the provisions of subsection (3) of section 3 of the African Marriages Act *(Chapter 238)*, the fact that the marriage has not been registered does not affect the issue of custody - *Haruzi Munyekete* v *Mberikwazvi Chirume* 1971 AAC 27; but the fact of the existence of the marriage must be proved before the father can claim any rights to custody - *Bessie* v *Ruwashe* 1970 AAC 48. The court is not bound by any agreement of the parents as to custody. It must decide for itself what is in the best interests of the children - *Maria* v *Linos* 1970 AAC 46.

Where there is nothing to show that such a procedure would be contrary to natural justice or morality or that the best interests of the child would be adversely affected, a husband may be awarded custody of an adulterine child - *Francisca a/b Simon* v *Matope* 1953 SRN 350. However, the husband is not obliged to claim custody of an adulterine child and may decline to have anything to do with it - *Kanyuka Sixpence* v *Egisita a/b John Hawker* 1967 AAC 37. Equally, notwithstanding the exercise by the husband of his claim, if the court considers it in the best interests of the child, it may award custody to the mother - *Kamangira* v *Jengera and Murapi* 1940 SRN 92.

A grievous wrong done by a husband to his wife's family will debar him (or his family if he is dead) from claiming any rights arising from the marriage, including custody of the children - *Simbodza* v *Maviyo* 1955 SRN 782. And in Shangaan custom, a man who kills his child forfeits all rights to the custody of his other children by the same wife - *Hlomani* v *Mjayi and Mawengi* 1933 SRN 53. In Vamanyika custom a man forfeits all rights to his children if he repudiates his wife for no good reason or no sufficient reason - *Shingirayi* v *Chiwonesu* 1953 SRN 342.

Where the parties are foreigners from a matrileaneal society but have married and had children in Rhodesia, the issue of custody is settled in accordance with Rhodesian customary law - *Tabiya and Sineki* v *Nyama* 1963 CAR 15 (from Nyasaland); *Kangachere* v *David Khondowe* 1963 CAR 33 (from Zambia); *Ides and Goliat* v *Getson* 1963 CAR 79 (from Nyasaland).

In matrimonial disputes concerning the custody of children, the woman must be assisted by her father or guardian - *Julia* v *Matapulaye* 1952 SRN 306. Conversely, the father of the husband has no *locus standi* to enforce a custody order in favour of his son - *Juliet Munemo and Charakupa* v *Runguta* 1955 SRN 475.

Guardianship

By customary law, the guardianship of a child rests with the father unless there are special reasons debarring him therefrom - *Mabande* v *Masiya* 1959 SRN 630. Clearly, guardianship cannot be awarded to a person who is himself subject to the guardianship of another - *Musekiwa Mutsonzwa* v *Big Boy a/b Kefasi Masosha* 1976 AAC 38. This is so notwithstanding the order as to custody, and care should be taken not to confuse the two - *Ally Musaka* v *Elizabeth Matope* 1959 SRN 622.

Maintenance

When custody of the children is awarded to the mother thereof on the dissolution of the marriage, the father should be ordered to pay maintenance for the children while they remain in the custody of the mother - *Malipiti and Julia* v *Kandiro* 1946 SRN 94 - and the amount of the maintenance ordered should be a fixed and definite sum - *Gilbert* v *Chandiyangana* 1949 SRN 220. In fixing this sum, the court must inquire into the means of the person against whom the order is sought and, in terms of subsection (2) of section 6 of the Maintenance Act (*Chapter 35*), satisfy itself that the person concerned is able to contribute to the maintenance - *Anthony Muchabaiwa Marimo* v *Adelheid Marimo* 1976 AAC 26. In addition, the judgment should specify clearly the names and ages of the children, the date when custody begins and ends, the amount of maintenance in respect of each child, and the person to whom the maintenance is to be paid - *Elisa and Musonda* v *Lavu* 1949 SRN 228; *Guwanzewe* v *Alica and Murapa* 1952 SRN 299 (sex of each child also to be recorded); *Julia* v *Matapulaye* 1952 SRN 306. Even if custody is awarded to the father, but for the present it is too young to leave its mother, then she should be awarded maintenance while she retains it - *Miki* v *Emely and Mbgadzawa* 1952 SRN 291. And if the husband thereafter fails to take custody, he may be liable for increased maintenance - *Bachi Vela* v *M'Bayiwa Jack* 1953 SRN 361.

In matters of maintenance, customary law should be applied unless the justice of the case requires otherwise - *Chikosi* v *Chikosi (2)* 1973 (1) RLR 199 (GD). Accordingly although a father who has paid *lobolo* in full and was not the culpable cause of the dissolution of the marriage is not normally liable to his father-in-law for maintenance of his children, circumstances may dictate that he should be so liable - *Mkarange* v *Tamange* 1949 SRN 207. However, it is established custom that a father-in-law cannot claim maintenance in respect of the period during which he holds *lobolo* and during the subsistence of the marriage - *Zira* v *Pompey* 1946 SRN 137; *David Milase* v *Witness* 1958 SRN 486. Neither is a person who has kept the children from their guardian against his will entitled to maintenance - *Ginza* v *Johannes* 1936 SRN 92. On the other hand a father-in-law may be entitled to claim maintenance if, in the absence of the husband from the marital home, his father refuses to maintain them - *Mado* v *Skudamedzi* 1942 SRN 193; *Petros Sithole* v *Moses Rukunda* 1976 AAC 6.

A rearing fee should be paid at the date of dissolution of the marriage - *Moses* v *Nobula and Charlton* 1944 SRN 38 - but not if the wife incited the child in her care to desert her husband, to whom custody had been awarded on dissolution of the marriage - *Margaret* v *Amon* 1946 SRN 90. Neither can a father-in-law recover a rearing fee from the husband where the wife deserts the marital home with the children and goes to her father, who refuses to return either her or the children to the husband, on the grounds that *lobolo* has not been paid - *Nendaya and Tigere* v *Zidenga* 1955 SRN 499.

Owing to changing conditions the archaic token payment of a beast as rearing fee may well be disproportionate to the actual expenses of the party who fed and clothed the children for a number of years. Consequently, rearing fees are no longer calculated on the basis of a beast, and a more realistic approach should be made - *Sam Msonko* v *Mutuswu* 1963 CAR 7.

(3) ILLEGITIMATE CHILDREN

Custody and guardianship

The basic rule of customary law is that a natural father has no right to the custody of his illegitimate child, notwithstanding that he may have paid damages for seduction of its mother. The father or guardian of the mother has an absolute discretion as to whether he will allow the father of the child to have custody thereof - *Gunda* v *Alexander* 1973 AAC 35; *Robert* v *Abraham* 1952 SRN 293. The mother's father or guardian may relinquish custody on payment by the child's father of *muripo* or *chiredzwa* but until this payment has been made it is the mother's father or guardian who is responsible for the maintenance of the child, not the child's father - *Moses Mvenge* v *Emma Tafura* 1974 AAC 9. If, however, the mother's father or guardian has agreed to accept *lobolo* and maintenance or rearing fee, then the right to the child rests with its father, provided the figure has been agreed upon, and the mother's father or guardian cannot recant on the agreement - *Maida and Stephan* v *Libona* 1964 AAC 32; *Siamosa* v *Kadembo* 1953 SRN 325. There is no obligation on the mother's father or guardian to accept the payments offered to obtain custody by the child's father - the matter is solely a matter for his discretion - regard being had to the child's moral and material welfare - *Muramwa* v *Majoni* 1947 SRN 165; *Sanislayi* v *Sophia and Jackson* 1951 SRN 279. The natural father of a child becomes liable to maintenance only if he is awarded custody - *Kainos* v *Tazvivinga* 1973 AAC 28. Similarly, he has no claim to its guardianship and is not legally liable to pay maintenance for it in terms of section 6(2) of the Maintenance Act *(Chapter 35)* - *Fordson Manduna* v *Clara Khanye* 1977 AAC 9. When he is not granted custody, his liability ceases with the payment of damages for seduction. This arrangement has been held not to be contrary to natural justice or morality - *In re Robert* 1953 SR 47.

The father or guardian of the mother cannot be compelled to relinquish custody to the father of the child on the grounds that the sum he sets as *chiredzwa* is unreasonably high, for the setting of such a high sum may be tantamount to a refusal to accept the *chiredzwa*, a matter which, in any event, is within his discretion - *Ndabanengi* v *Tutai* 1953 SRN 329. An order for custody was refused on the ground of non-entitlement when it was ascertained that at the time of the seduction of the child's mother, the man was validly married to another woman by Christian rites - *Michael Chikololere* v *Lameck Gabuza* 1969 AAC 38.

Notwithstanding the above basic rule of customary law, the prime consideration should be the best interests of the child, both as regards custody and guardianship, and the court should hear evidence on this aspect of the matter - *Adinisi* v *George* 1969 AAC 36.

A similar principle applies in relation to adulterine children - *Kamangira* v *Jengera and Murapi* 1940 SRN 92 - although generally speaking the custody of such a child rests with the husband of the erring wife. If this general rule is departed from and the seducer obtains custody then it is almost invariably as a result of agreement, and the claim may be laid by the seducer tendering cattle - *Lydia* v *Musumbu* 1939 SRN 74. In *Vela* v *Mondinika and Magutsa* 1936 SRN 171 it was held to be contrary to natural justice to refuse to accept a reasonable offer by the child's father.

It is established custom that a man has no claim to his incestuous child - *Munzara* v *Muskwati* 1953 SRN 402. Neither can a man lay claim to an unborn child of which he is not the father - *Mungazi* v *Chimbande* 1937 SRN 1 - and where the natural father fails to pay *lobolo* before his death, his heir cannot claim that guardianship of the child vests in him - *Hlezipe* v *Kotosi* 1953 SRN 323.

A claim for custody is usually made by one spouse against the other but in cases where paternity is in doubt, such a claim may be made against the person who actually has the child in his care - *Chidombgwe* v *Nyadakudjga* 1949 SRN 223.

Maternity expenses

Lying-in expenses may be included in the damages awarded for seduction but they should be properly proved, and this cannot be done until after the birth of the child - *De Souza* v *Munjoma* 1951 SRN 260. Such expenses may include maintenance of the girl - *Nyoni* v *Mamova* 1949 SRN 216.

Paternity

Once it has been shown that the man and the girl did have sexual intercourse and thereafter he is named as the father of a child born subsequently, a presumption of paternity arises and the onus is on him to prove that he is not the child's father - *Charles Ndhlovu* v *Mketwa Ndhlovu* 1971 AAC 37. However, before judgment is given in favour of the girl, there must be credible corroboration for her evidence that the defendant is the father of her child. In cases of doubt, judgment should be given in favour of the defendant - *Musonoki* v *Jacopo* 1962 SRN 12; *Stanley Machakanja* v *Martin* 1953 CAR 19.

If, in a divorce action, the paternity of a child born in wedlock is cast in doubt but there is no evidence to exclude the possibility that the husband is the father, the maxim *pater est quam nuptiae demonstrant* should be applied and custody awarded to the husband - *Sheneti* v *Sadock* 1961 SRN 15. A similar presumption of legitimacy will arise where a married woman gives birth to a child before marriage but no dispute as to paternity is brought until the subsequent divorce proceedings are heard - *Elizabeth and Mzeze* v *Gwandibva* 1941 SRN 121. Where a man lives with a woman, pays damages for seduction, and then marries her, there is a presumption that he is the father of any child born after the marriage. Both she and her father or guardian are estopped from later denying the husband's paternity - *Hlale* v *Dziyakwi* 1938 SRN 34.

In Ndebele custom, a man has the right to recognize the paternity of an illegitimate child of his daughter by accepting from the seducer cattle as *lobolo umtwana*. His decision to do so is, however, within his discretion and he may refuse such recognition by refusing to accept the cattle tendered - *Manikisi* v *Sikonwane Madubege* 1934 SRN 72 - although this discretion is open to qualification - *Sambo* v *Moyo and Makumalo* 1939 SRN 58.

CHAPTER IV

DELICT

REAL AND PERSONAL RIGHTS

A. DELICT

B. REAL RIGHTS

Section 1. *Ownership*

Section 2. *Succession*

Section 3. *Personal Rights*

A. DELICT

Accident

In order to sustain a claim for actual damages for personal injury, the plaintiff must prove malice. Where injury is caused to another unwittingly, in the course of social contact, or arises out of an accident directly attributable to some rough action, the usual remedy is known as *ushamavanga*, a token payment of, say, a goat, by way of atonement - *George* v *Garaza* 1948 SRN 187.

Animals

Where death or injury is caused to any person by a domestic animal, through excitement or vice without liability attaching to the owner thereof, in Vamanyika custom no action lies against the owner. However, in such circumstances recourse can be had to the common law. The only action in customary law is for the animal to be surrendered to the chief, to be killed and its meat distributed to the family of the injured person - *Chakara* v *Goro* 1959 SRN 644.

Assault

An individual right of action for assault is competent in customary law - *Keresiah and Jack* v *Martha and Mugweni Makimba* 1958 SRN 551 - but there is little conflict between such law and the common law on the question of liability. The plaintiff may claim in respect of compensation for (1) actual expenditure and pecuniary loss; (2) disfigurement, pain and suffering, and loss of general health and the amenities of life; and (3) future expenses and loss of earning capacity - *Nyovane* v *Murongwana* 1956 SRN 503. A woman suing for damages for personal injury cannot include in her claim any loss of her services to her husband - *Meri* v *Merita* 1966 AAC 53 - although special damages may be claimed - *Machokomere* v *Tapfuma* 1969 AAC 22.

Damages can be assessed only on the basis of the evidence before the court, to permit it to award such damages as it thinks reasonable in the circumstances. Therefore, evidence must be called on all the aspects upon which the claim is based - *Rudia and Enock* v *Ignatius Rangarirayi* 1964 AAC 66 - and the amount of damages sought must be proved in evidence - *Funnwell* v *Simon* 1970 AAC 25. Actual assessment should be in accordance with the common law and, accordingly, may be awarded jointly and severally - *Dominic & another* v *John Mujongonda* 1970 AAC 6 - and provocation may be a relevant factor - *Amon Nyamupfukudza* v *Dorothy a/b Chirekeni* 1968 AAC 1; *Nyamayare* v *Chamunorgwa* 1958 SRN 530.

Children - liability for acts of

A parent's liability for the wrongdoings of his children is wider in customary law than it is under the common law, and a parent may be personally liable for the injury caused by his child - *Matiyenga and Mamire* v *Chinamura & others* 1958 SRN 55. Accordingly, the proper person to proceed against is the father of the child - *Stewart a/b Patrick* v *Chigumbura* 1971 AAC 35 (although this does not apply to an emancipated child who has established a home for himself, is economically independent and physically an adult - *Edwin Momeshora* v *Kennie Chirume* 1971 AAC 30). Thus, the fathers of herdboys were held responsible for their children driving cattle over a cliff, to punish them for trespassing on cultivated lands, and in *Ruwo* v *Rabson* 1965 AAC 20 the father of a child who had caused serious personal injury to another child was found liable in respect of the injury caused. Such liability does not, however, extend to injury caused by a child who is no longer under his care and control - *Violet and Mahlaule* v *Girison* 1964 AAC 43; *Takawadiyi* v *Munyukwi Siyawamwaya* 1969 AAC 47. Proof of malice or an intention to cause injury is an essential ingredient of a successful action - *Andrea* v *Mangarayi* 1966 AAC 32. The general rule of liability of parents for the wrongdoings of their children applies equally to the liability of a husband for the wrongdoing of his wife - *Muchechesi* v *Seven* 1969 AAC 43 - and may include injury done by a wife to the property of her husband - *Time Chichetu* v *Mrs A Chichetu* 1977 AAC 27.

Defamation

An action for damages for defamation lies in customary law, unless the words used were addressed to someone in authority in good faith and without express malice. Words spoken lightly or in a heated quarrel and later withdrawn, or common abuse, should not form the basis of an action. An indication whether words are defamatory is whether they would alter the attitude of the members of his social group towards the person maligned, and so endanger his tribal status and the harmony of his social life - *Lesitoni* v *Eniyasi* 1966

AAC 14. It is an essential element of a cause of action for defamation that the words used should be 'of the plaintiff'. If they are not, the plaintiff is not defamed and, consequently, has no cause of action - *Henry Bwerudza* v *Samuel Muzunye Mhlanga* 1959 SRN 628. Moreover, if it is not shown that *animus injuriandi* was present, then the claim must fail - *Gatsi Kasukwere* v *Josaiah Danarembgwa* 1961 SRN 7.

Publication for the public benefit constitutes a good defence to an action - *Swondo* v *Gombingo* 1967 AAC 16 - as does proof that the defamatory statement was true, although the onus in both cases is on the defendant - *Richard Mpofu* v *Daisy Dube a/b Hambi Dube* 1967 AAC 21.

A person who makes a defamatory statement is not liable if such statement was made on a privileged occasion - *Rabson* v *Makoti* 1969 AAC 54. The scope of what is a privileged occasion varies but, provided the occasion was not abused, a statement to a person in authority is privileged - *Shangwa* v *Jona Virimayi* 1969 AAC 45; so are statements during court proceedings - *Mariyana* v *Musarurwa Katema* 1971 AAC 13 - allegations at a preliminary family *dare* - *Morgen Makumbe* v *Mabugu* 1965 AAC 52 - or in a chief's court - *Elinah Ndebele and Fani Ndebele* v *Pitoli Ncube* 1965 AAC 44 - or a complaint incorporating a defamatory statement made to mission authorities - *Elinah Ndebele's* case *(supra)*- and to a person who otherwise has a legitimate interest in receiving it - *John W G Sojini* v *Jokoniah Nyati* 1972 AAC 14.

When considering the quantum of damages in cases of defamation, the most important element is the nature of the defamation - *Tasara Antonio* v *Romos* 1962 SRN 1. And, if two different defamatory allegations are made in one action, it is legitimate to assess damages separately for each - *Terera* v *Sithole and Sithole* 1964 AAC 38.

Malicious and Wrongful Legal Proceedings

It is incumbent upon a plaintiff who brings an action for wrongful and malicious proceedings, to prove -

(*a*) that there was no ground for the original judgment; and

(*b*) that the original proceedings were instituted maliciously; and

(*c*) that the original proceedings had been instituted without reasonable and probable cause - *Cyprian Hamandishe* v *Soda Mupambari* 1968 AAC 16.

In order to prove a claim for malicious prosecution, the plaintiff must show that the defendant was actuated by some improper motive, and acting without reasonable cause instituted or instigated the prosecution against him - *Prisca* v *Mutandizi Maxwell Makwara* 1976 AAC 9.

Negligence

An owner of cattle has a duty to ensure that such cattle do not trespass on another's land, and may be liable in negligence if they do - *Meyi Ndhlovu* v *Geula Ndhlovu* 1971 AAC 22.

In an action for negligence, the summons must allege the negligence complained of and certain details of when and where it took place - *Try Again Bus Service and Semu Moyo NO* v *James Moyo* 1964 AAC 26.

It is no bar to an action for negligence arising out of a motor accident that the parties knew the venture during which the accident happened was prohibited by statute - *Pikani Simeon* v *Patrick Gufu* 1959 SRN 620. In proving damages for injury, evidence must be adduced to show that charges for repairs are fair and reasonable - *Daniel* v *Agness Tinarwo* 1966 AAC 39.

B. REAL RIGHTS

(I) OWNERSHIP

Immovable property

The ownership of immovable property is a form of ownership not known to customary law - *Komo* v *Leboho and Holmes NO* 1935 SR 86. Consequently, disputes concerning the ownership of immovable property fall to be decided by common law.

Movable property

Customary law relating to the ownership of property by women has been referred to in Chapter III, as a matter that, from time to time, has aroused controversy or given rise to dispute. In other aspects, the ownership of movable property appears to have given little difficulty and such disputes as have arisen relate almost entirely to the disputed ownership of cattle.

On marriage, the ownership of *lobolo* cattle passes from the son-in-law to his father-in-law - *Mbidzani* v *Diki and Siya* 1938 SRN 21. Similarly, in Ndebele custom, when the heir to a deceased estate points out cattle at the *ukubuyisa* ceremony, as the share due to a relative, a form of *longa manu* delivery, ownership also passes immediately - *Magwisi* v *Kombayi* 1947 SRN 177.

In customary law an action lies against a herdsman with whom cattle are left by the owner thereof, to account for the cattle and any increase in the herd. However, no award can be made if the increase is neither ascertained nor ascertainable - *Munyengetergwa* v *Katapa* 1938 SRN 43. Neither can he complain that the herdsman has failed in his customary duty of reporting any increase or producing the hides of all animals that have died if there is no direct evidence of any increase or deaths - *Manuka* v *Makanyesi* 1942 SRN 162. Moreover, where a plaintiff sues for the return of cattle left in the possession of a herdsman, he must be able to show how many cattle are to be returned to him - *Francisco* v *Sikupa* 1940 SRN 82.

(2) SUCCESSION

Intestate

Subsection (1) of section 69 of the Administration of Estates Act *(Chapter 301)* provides:

> '(1) If any African who has contracted a marriage according to African law and custom or who, being unmarried, is the offspring of parents married according to African law and custom, dies intestate his estate shall be administered and distributed according to the customs and usages of the tribe or people to which he belonged.'

Subsection (2) of this section provides that in the event of any controversy or dispute arising among the relatives as to the distribution of property, the provincial or senior magistrate of the province shall determine such dispute according to customary law. Subsections (3) and (4) provide for appeals, and the procedure for such appeals, from a determination of such a magistrate to the Appellate Division of the High Court. Subsection (5) dispenses with the issues of letters of administration from the Master of the High Court, unless in any particular case the district commissioner requests the appointment of an executor dative. Accordingly, a district commissioner's court and the Court of Appeal for African Civil Cases has no jurisdiction in respect of the determination of disputes brought in terms of subsection (2) to (4) of section 69 of the Act.

The general rule of customary law is that the eldest son is the natural heir of his deceased father - *Muhango* v *France* 1940 SRN 100. This right to inherit is established once it is shown that the father has paid *lobolo* or that the son pays after his death - *Wafani* v *Nyoni* 1962 SRN 25. More particularly, the heir is he to whom his deceased father's name was given - *Mpani* v *Msetshwa* 1958 SRN 557. He does so on the principle that he succeeds to his father's name and exercises control over his father's 'house' for the benefit of its members - *Bezai* v *Tamisayi* 1969 AAC 58. The general rule, however, is subject to qualifications and exceptions. Thus, a brother of the deceased may succeed in the absence of male issue - *Jamu* v *Jim and Takaziweyi* 1939 SRN 49; *Duma* v *Madidi* 1918 SR 59. Again, in Ndebele custom, the heir is the eldest surviving son of the principle or 'great house' (the 'great' wife must be *intombi*) - *Mdujulwa* v *Madhliwa* 1945 SRN 63.

Moreover, Ndebele (and Fingo - *Gibson* v *Mbishe* 1949 SRN 225) custom allows a father, for good and sufficient reasons to disinherit his heir. Proper reasons for so doing include shedding the blood of a member of the family, insanity or a very bad character. Before such steps are taken, however, all members of the family should be consulted in the presence of the chief and a formal and public declaration which includes the appointment of a successor should be made - *Moyo* v *Moyo* 1959 SRN 641.

An heir who takes his father's name and inherits his estate is responsible for *lobolo* paid to his deceased father, even though the *lobolo* was used by his brother and, consequently, is the person against whom an action for the return of the *lobolo* may be properly brought - *Maworera* v *Chavanduka* 1941 SRN 119. Family expenses incurred and paid, as between the heir as head of the family and his younger brother, are not reclaimable - *Samson* v *Justin* 1952 SRN 344.

Generally speaking, no female may inherit property, more especially where the deceased leaves children - *Juniah and Juniasi* v *Nawa* 1949 SRN 210 - and there is no provision in customary law whereby the sister of the deceased is entitled either to inherit or distribute her brother's estate - *Munzara* v *Nerera* 1944 SRN 24. However, in certain circumstances a widow may inherit as trustee for the deceased's eldest son - *Sipamehle* v *Dube* 1940 SRN 79; particularly in Ndebele custom, such a form of inheritance is not uncommon - *Mabigwa* v *Matibini* 1946 SRN 117.

A claim against a deceased's estate must be made at the *kurowa guwa* ceremony unless there are strong reasons for a failure to do so - *Pisira* v *Enoki Sonokele* 1954 SRN 446; *Gideon* v *Tawadzadza* 1946 SRN 108; *Mhlaba* v *Makuhlane* 1947 SRN 180. The onus is on the claimant *Muhango* v *France* 1940 SRN 100. No claim can be made fo fees for digging a grave or assisting at a burial - *Willie* v *Matafi* 1941 SRN 126. The heir is entitled to custody and guardianship of the deceased's children, provided he is suitable and any claims for outstanding *lobolo* have been settled - *Nau* v *Mazwane* 1946 SRN 128.

Testate

Notwithstanding the provisions of customary law, in terms of section 3 of the African Wills Act *(Chapter 240)*, any African married by Christian or civil rites may make provision for the guardianship of his children by will. If no such provision is made then, in terms of section 4, any person lawfully interested in the children may seek an order for their guardianship from the district commissioner. Such orders, in terms of section 5, are appealable.

Section 6 of the Act provides that immovable property or any rights thereto may be disposed of by will. But if there is no such disposition then the heir at African law, in terms of section 7, succeeds in his individual capacity to such immovable property and any rights thereto. The phrase 'heir at African law' is accorded its ordinary meaning, that is, the person who is entitled to succeed to the property of the deceased. Usually this will be the eldest son of the deceased, but if under customary law some other person is entitled to succeed then that person may be regarded as the 'heir at African law' within the meaning of section 7 of the Act - *Matambo* v *Matambo* 1969 (2) RLR 154 (AD).

By section 10 of the Act, any question or dispute concerning any will or the subject-matter thereof is settled by the district commissioner, subject to the right of appeal against a decision made by him. The Act, by virtue of the provisions of section 11, should not be construed as substituting a testamentary successor as the general heir of the testator. When customary law cannot properly be applied to matters of inheritance and succession, the common law prevails - *Dokotera* v *The Master of the High Court* 1957 R&N 697 (SR).

(3) PERSONAL RIGHTS

Carriers

A bus conductor is merely the bus owner's agent and unless it can be proved that he performed a wrongful act not based upon the contract between the plaintiff and his principal, no action lies against him for loss of the plaintiff's goods - *Ringirai* v *Changara* 1970 AAC 9; *John Sachikonye* v *Nyaradzai* 1969 AAC 33; although an action against a bus owner is perfectly competent - *Elias Machida* v *Philemon* 1964 AAC 29 - for the common law principle of the absolute liability of professional carriers to deliver goods to the consignee subject only to the defences of *vis major* and *damnum fatale* applies to customary law - *Tangwara* v *Tlili* 1960 SRN 680. Similarly, a bus conductor who undertakes personally to deliver goods is liable for non-delivery - *Titus Dube* v *Munyoro William* 1971 AAC 6.

In view of the exceptional diligence demanded of carriers, damages claimed against them must be scrutinized closely and proved in detail - *Ntubeni Bus Service* v *Vamu* 1962 SRN 20.

A contract of carriage for hire or reward is illegal unless the owner of the vehicle is in possession of a valid road service permit. It is therefore unenforceable. A court dealing with such a claim is obliged itself to raise this point to avoid the enforcement of an illegal contract - *Hora* v *Maendaenda* 1970 AAC 13 - for the whole transaction is illegal and void - *Musarurgwa* v *Magende* 1959 SRN 625.

Deposit

Contracts of deposit fall to be decided by the common law unless the justice of the case otherwise requires. Because of the vagueness of customary law in such matters this has been the practice for many years. Under the common law, therefore, no claim lies against a person who has accepted the care of property without making a charge for doing so if that property is lost, provided no negligence can be attributed to him - *Farwell Chamboko* v *Jonasi Nyamayovo* 1972 AAC 1; *Edward Jelasi* v *Irene* 1971 AAC 3.

Illegal contracts - generally

A contract may be set aside on the grounds of coercion, if the following five essentials are present -

(1) actual violence or reasonable fear;

(2) the fear must be caused by some real threat to person or family;

(3) the evil threatened must be imminent or inevitable;

(4) the threat must be *contra bonos mores*;

(5) the person threatened must have acted on the violence or threat to his detriment - *Richard Shumba* v *Tsakayirenzi* 1973 AAC 7.

In terms of the Medical, Dental and Allied Professions Act *(Chapter 224)*, only registered medical practitioners are entitled to sue for payment of fees for treating persons as doctors. A person who is not a registered medical practitioner may not treat a person as a doctor and any claim for payment for such treatment is not recoverable at law - *Joshua Murigwa* v *Johnson Mudawanhu* 1970 AAC 11.

Purchase and sale

A person who alleges payment of a debt must prove that such payment occurred - *Gideon Heya* v *George Tinargwo* 1973 AAC 26.

APPENDIX I

DISTRICT COMMISSIONER'S COURT RULES
R.G.N. Nos 1151/1973; 146/1975

ARRANGEMENT OF RULES

Order 1

PRELIMINARY

Rule

1. Title
2. Interpretation of terms.

Order 2

COMMENCEMENT OF PROCEEDINGS

3. Receiving of claims.
4. Date and place of hearing.
5. Notice to defendant.
6. Securing attendance of witnesses.
7. Service of process.

Order 3

CONDUCT OF PROCEEDINGS

8. Representation of parties.
9. Record of proceedings.
10. Reading of claim.
11. Swearing in.
12. Calling of evidence.
13. Cross-examination.
14. Examination of witness by interrogatories.
15. Address.
16. Plaintiff in default.
17. Defendant in default.
18. Restitution of conjugal rights.
19. Proceedings.

Order 4

JUDGMENTS AND THEIR ENFORCEMENT

Rule

20. Judgments.
21. Messengers.
22. Execution of judgments.
23. Attachment of property.
24. Additional provisions relating to the attachment of immovable property.
25. Garnishee orders.

Order 5

APPEALS

26. Appeal procedure.

Order 6

COSTS, FEES AND DEPARTURE FROM RULES

27. Costs.
28. Fees.
29. Departure from rules.

Order 7

REPEAL OF EXISTING RULES

30. Repeals.

Schedules

First Schedule: Forms

Second Schedule: Fees

Third Schedule: Repeals

Order 1

PRELIMINARY

Title

1. These rules may be cited as the District Commissioner's Court Rules, 1973.

Interpretation of terms

2. In these rules -

'clerk of court' means the clerk of the district commissioner's court appointed for that purpose by the district commissioner.

'court' means the court of the district commissioner unless otherwise stated;

'Court of Appeal' means the Court of Appeal for African Civil Cases;

'form' means a form prescribed in the First Schedule;

'messenger of court' means a messenger of the district commissioner's court appointed for that purpose by the district commissioner and commonly called the *chikonzi* or *sikonzi*;

'record book' means the civil record book prescribed as form DCC1 in the First Schedule.

Order 2

COMMENCEMENT OF PROCEEDINGS

Receiving of claims

3. (1) A claim shall be lodged with the clerk of the district commissioner's court which has jurisdiction to hear the matter, during normal office hours and at

such place as the district commissioner may direct.

(2) Upon lodging a claim in terms of subrule (1), the plaintiff shall tender the appropriate claim fee and the appropriate messenger's fees in accordance with subrule (3) of rule 21 and the clerk of court shall -

(a) draw up the appropriate summons; and
(b) complete the record jacket form DCC 5 and record thereon the address for service of documents of both parties.

Date and place of hearing

(4) After drawing up the summons for the plaintiff in terms of rule 3, the clerk of the court shall appoint and specify a convenient time, day and place for the hearing of the claim and shall notify the plaintiff accordingly.

Notice to defendant

(5) (1) The messenger shall serve on the defendant a summons on form DCC 2 setting out the particulars referred to in subrule (2) and shall warn the defendant that the address at which service was effected upon him shall be deemed to be his address for service of documents unless he notifies the clerk of court to the contrary within seven days.

(2) The messenger of court shall, so far as practical, inform the defendant of the nature and grounds of the claim against him, and the date, time and place at which he and his witnesses, if any, are required to appear before the court to answer such claim.

(3) In every case the messenger shall, as soon as service has been effected, enter a return of service with the clerk of the court on the reverse of form DCC 2.

(4) A defendant may consent to judgment on the full amount of the claim against him by -

(a) signing the form of consent endorsed on the original summons; or
(b) notifying the clerk of court of such consent at any time before the time appointed for the hearing.

Securing attendance of witnesses

6. (1) The process for compelling the attendance of any person to give evidence shall be by subpoena, on form DCC 3, served on such person by the messenger of court.

(2) A subpoena shall be issued at the instance of either party who requires the attendance of any witness, on payment of the prescribed fee, together with the appropriate messenger's fee in accordance with subrule (3) of rule 21 and any re-imbursement which may be required to be paid into court in terms of subrule (5).

(3) A witness shall be entitled to reimbursement of reasonable expenses incurred by him in travelling to and from the court by the party who requires his attendance.

(4) A witness shall be entitled to be re-imbursed the cost of his detention for each night he is obliged to be away from his home as a result of being subpoenaed as a witness by the party who requires his attendance.

(5) The district commissioner may require all reimbursements to which a witness may be entitled in terms of subrules (3) and (4) to be paid into court before the issue of the subpoena by the party who requires the attendance of such witness.

Service of document

7. (1) If it appears to the district commissioner that personal service of any document cannot be effected, he may give instructions for service of the document in any manner provided in section 34 of the Interpretation Act *(Chapter 1)*.

(2) When the court is satisfied that service of a document cannot be effected in any other manner prescribed by these rules and that the action is within its jurisdiction the court may make an order authorizing service to be effected in such manner as may be stated in such order, including notice by advertisement in substitution for personal service.

Order 3

CONDUCT OF PROCEEDINGS

Representation of parties

8. (1) Any party to a case may be represented before the court by an advocate or an attorney.

(2) If a party dies, or, in the opinion of the court, is incompetent to continue an action, the action shall be stayed until such time as the court is satisfied that there is an heir, guardian or other competent person to take over the legal responsibilities of such party or until such incompetence shall have ceased to exist.

Record of proceedings

9. (1) In every case the district commissioner shall take down the proceedings in writing, and shall also note all relevant facts and objections which either party may desire to be recorded.

(2) The proceedings in the court shall be conducted and the evidence shall be delivered in such language or languages as in the opinion of the court seems most conducive to the ends of justice.

(3) The records of the court shall be kept in the English language, and when the evidence is offered in a language other than English the district commissioner, in recording it, shall reduce such language to the English language.

(4) The record of the proceedings of each case shall be enclosed in a jacket in the form DCC 5.

Reading of claim

10. (1) If the claim has not been withdrawn or satisfied by consent to judgment, the district commissioner shall cause the parties to be called at the time appointed for the hearing, or so soon thereafter as is convenient.

10. (2) After the parties have been called in terms of subrule (1) the court shall -

(a) ask the plaintiff if he agrees to the terms of the claim lodged in terms of rule 3 or if he wishes it to be amended; and

(b) put the claim, with amendments, if any, to the defendant; and

(c) call upon the defendant to admit or deny the facts alleged in such claim; and

(d) record the plea of the defendant, and any counterclaim which the defendant desires to make; and

(e) record the plaintiff's reply to the plea.

(3) After the court has complied with subrule (2), either party may for sufficient cause request a postponement or adjournment, which may, in the discretion of the court, be granted.

(4) If the defendant admits the claim in full, the court shall satisfy itself that the claim is valid, and judgement may thereafter be given as if the defendant had consented to judgment as provided in subrule (4) of rule 5.

Swearing in

11. (1) A witness shall be sworn by the district commissioner, according to the form of religion which such witness professes, to tell the truth, the whole truth and nothing but the truth, and shall thereafter be examined orally:

Provided that all persons entitled by law to affirm instead of taking an oath may so affirm.

(2) Notwithstanding the provisions of subrule (1), any person produced for the purpose of giving evidence, and is found not to understand the nature or recognize the obligations of an oath or

affirmation, may be admitted to give evidence without being sworn or making an affirmation:

Provided that before any such person proceeds to give evidence the district commissioner before whom he is offered as a witness shall admonish him to speak the truth, the whole truth, and nothing but the truth.

Calling of evidence

12. If the defendant denies the facts set forth in the claim, the plaintiff subject to the provisions of subrule (1) of rule 29, shall proceed to produce the evidence upon which his claim is founded, and thereafter the defendant shall produce the evidence in support of his plea.

Cross-examination

13. (1) Each party, together with his witnesses, shall be liable to cross-examination by the opposite party, and the district commissioner shall, in every case, at the conclusion of the evidence-in-chief of a witness, inquire whether the opposite party desires to exercise the right of cross-examination.

(2) Each party shall be entitled to re-examine on the evidence given in cross-examination and the district commissioner shall in every case on the conclusion of the cross-examination inquire whether the right to re-examine is to be exercised.

(3) The court shall have the right to question any witness and may at its own instance receive the evidence of any person whom it regards as likely to give material evidence who is within the precincts of the court and wishing to give evidence.

Examination of witness by interrogatories

14 (1) When a witness is resident in a district other than that of the court, the court may, upon the request of either party and after hearing the other

party, if it considers such a course desirable, and on payment of the prescribed fee, the subpoena fee and the messenger's fee, and on approval of such interrogatories as either party desires to have put to such witness, frame and forward them to the district commissioner of the district where such witness is resident.

(2) The district commissioner who receives interrogatories in terms of subrule (1) shall forthwith subpoena the witness to appear in his court and upon his appearance therein shall -

(a) put to the witness the interrogatories and all other questions calculated to obtain full and true answers to the interrogatories;

(b) take down in writing the evidence of the witness;

(c) transmit the evidence of the witness, certified as correct, to the district commissioner from whom the interrogatories were received.

(3) Evidence received in terms of subrule (2) shall be admissible as evidence in the court of the district commissioner who framed the interrogatories.

Address

15. On completion of the evidence, each party or his advocate or attorney in turn may address the court in support of his case.

Plaintiff in default

16 (1) If at the time fixed for the hearing of any case the defendant is present and the plaintiff is in default, the action shall be dismissed and the defendant shall be entitled to his costs.

(2) If the action is dismissed because of the default of the plaintiff in appearing, he may reopen the case on the payment of all costs awarded

against him in the original action and on tender of a fresh claim fee:

Provided that the court may at its discretion waive tender of a fresh claim fee.

Defendant in default

17. (1) If the defendant does not appear in court on the day and at the time he was summoned to appear in terms of rule 5, the court may, on being satisfied that the defendant has had due and sufficient notice to attend, proceed to hear the case of the plaintiff and may, subject to subrule (2) give judgment thereon, including costs, against the defendant:

Provided that -

(a) the court may in its discretion, before execution, require the plaintiff, together with a surety to be approved by the court, to give security for full restitution of the amount to be levied and raised under such judgment;

(b) the defendant may, at any time within two months from the date of the original judgment, request the court to have the proceedings reopened, and the court shall reopen the proceedings if satisfied that there was sufficient excuse for the default of the defendant on the day of hearing of the original suit and the defendant provides security to the satisfaction of the court for costs previously incurred by the plaintiff;

(c) if the case is not reopened in terms of proviso (b),any security required in terms of proviso (a) shall no longer be required.

(2) Where a claim is for custody or divorce, and the defendant is in default, a rule *nisi* shall be issued calling on the defendant to appear at a specified time and date failing which judgment may be given in his absence.

Restitution of conjugal rights

18. (1) In any action for restitution of conjugal rights the plaintiff may also claim a decree of divorce as well as other relief.

(2) Upon the hearing of the case, the court may order the restitution of conjugal rights and direct the defendant to show cause on a day to be named in such order, not being less than seven days after the day fixed for compliance with the order for restitution, why a decree of divorce or other relief desired should not be granted.

(3) If, upon the day fixed in terms of subrule (2), it is proved by affidavit or otherwise that the defendant, having been given due notice, has failed to comply with the order or restitution of conjugal rights, the court may grant a decree of divorce or make such other order as it deems just.

Proceedings

19. (1) Whenever it appears to the court that there is sufficient cause, the hearing of a case may be postponed or adjourned from time to time to any convenient day, time and place, which postponement or adjournment and the cause thereof shall be entered on the civil record jacket and in the record book.

(2) Where either of the parties is not present at the time when the postponement or adjournment is granted, such party shall be notified by the clerk of the court on form DCC 6 of the day, time and place to which the case has been postponed or adjourned.

(3) Subject to the provisions of subrule (4), a court may direct that -

(a) proceedings shall be held *in camera;*

(b) such person or classes of persons as the court may specify, other than officers of court or persons whose presence is necessary in connection with the proceedings, shall be excluded from the proceedings.

(4) The powers conferred on the court by subrule (3) shall be exercised only where the court considers it necessary or expedient to do so in the interests of justice, security, public order, public morality, the welfare of young persons or the protection of the private lives of persons concerned in the proceedints in question.

(5) Any direction in terms of subrule (3) may be reviewed or revoked by the court at any time.

Order 4

JUDGMENTS AND THEIR ENFORCEMENT

Judgments

20. (1) All judgments of the court shall be delivered in open court, and shall be recorded on the civil record jacket, form DCC 5, and in the record book, form DCC 1.

(2) The court may grant -

(a) judgment for the plaintiff in respect of his claim in so far as he has proved the same;

(b) judgment for the defendant in respect of his defence;

(c) absolution from the instance if it appears to the court that the evidence does not justify the court in giving judgment for either party;

(d) such judgment as to costs as may be just.

(3) The court may -

(a) subject to the provisions of rules 16 and 17, rescind or vary any judgment which was granted by it in the absence of the party against whom it was granted.

(b) rescind or vary any judgment granted by it which was void *ab origine* or was obtained by frand or by mistake on the part of either party;

(c) correct patent errors in any judgment in respect of which no appeal is pending.

(4) The powers given in subrule (3) may only be exercised after notice by the applicant to the other party or, if no application has been made, after notice to both parties, and any exercise of such power shall be subject to appeal.

Messengers

21. (1) The messengers of the court shall not receive any fees in connection with the service of process or in the performance of any other duties imposed by the court other than through the court.

(2) Every messenger of court shall, when performing any duty on behalf of the court, wear a distinguishing badge or uniform or carry a letter of authority signed by the district commissioner.

(3) A district commissioner shall fix a tariff of fees in respect of all services performed by a messenger of court.

(4) The messenger to whom process is entrusted for service or execution shall, without delay and in any event within twenty-one days of receipt of process by him -

(a) if he has effected service or execution, notify the clerk of the court that service or execution has been duly effected, stating the date and manner of service or the result of execution;

(b) if he has not effected service or execution, notify the clerk of the court that he has been unable to effect service or execution, stating the reason for such inability.

Execution of judgment

22. (1) The party in whose favour any judgment of the court has been given, and in respect of which execution has not been stayed in consequence of an appeal, may apply to the court to have such judgment executed.

(2) The court shall have regard to and execute all judgments, orders and decrees of the Court of Appeal as if they were its own judgments, orders and decrees.

Attachment of property

23. (1) The process of execution against property of any judgment of the court shall, subject to the provisions of rule 24, be by warrant, in the form of DCC 4, issued on payment of the prescribed fee and the messenger's fee.

(2) The warrant of execution shall be communicated to the messenger of court, directing him to attach so much of the property of the person against whom such warrant is granted as is necessary to satisfy the amount of the judgment and of such costs, including the costs of execution, as have been allowed against such person.

(3) Such process may be issued in respect of any person in whose favour any judgment has been given, if such judgment has not been satisfied, stayed or suspended.

(4) Such process may at any time, on payment of the fees incurred, be withdrawn or suspended by notice to the clerk of court by the party who has caused such process to be issued.

(5) Any alterations in such process shall be initialled by the clerk of court before such process is issued by him.

(6) Any such process shall be invalid if a person be incorrectly named therein as a party:

Provided that no such process shall be invalid merely by reason of the mis-spelling or minor errors in any name therein, or of any error which is not likely to mislead.

(7) Except where judgment has been entered by consent or default, a warrant of execution shall not be issued before the day following that on which the judgment is given:

Provided that a warrant of execution may be issued at the time of judgment with the special leave of the court on good cause being shown.

(8) The messenger to whom the warrant is communicated in terms of subrule (2) shall forthwith proceed to attach such property as directed by the court and shall notify the party against whom such execution is granted that the property attached is in satisfaction of the judgment of the court and of the costs of the case and that such property will be disposed of at a certain date not less than one month from the date of such attachment if the judgment, together with costs, is not sooner satisfied.

(9) The district commissioner may, if he deems fit, and with the consent of a person specified by him, order that any property attached in terms of subrule (8) shall be -

(a) stored by such specified person;

(b) in the case of livestock, grazed and kraaled by such specified person; and

(c) sold by such specified person in the normal course of his business;

and subject to the provisions of subrule (10), any fees charged for such storage, grazing or sale shall be costs in the execution.

(10) The fees to be charged in terms of subrule (9) shall be laid down by the district commissioner, following consultation with the person specified in

the order, at the date of the making of any order in terms of subrule (9).

(11) If the property is situated in a district other than that of the court in which the execution is granted, the warrant of execution may be transmitted to the district commissioner of such district for endorsement for execution therein.

(12) Where the judgment is given against a partnership, the partnership property shall first be exhausted, so far as it is known to the judgment creditor, before the judgment is executed against the separate property of the partners.

(13) If any property which is taken or is about to be taken in execution is claimed by any third party as his property, the clerk of the court shall, on receipt of such claim, forthwith give notice of such claim to the execution creditor.

(14) If the execution creditor admits the claim made by a third party in terms of subrule (13) and, within two days of the receipt by him of such notice, informs the clerk of the court accordingly, the execution creditor shall not be liable for any costs, fees or expenses incurred thereafter in respect of the property so claimed and the district commissioner may withdraw from possession of such property.

(15) If the judgment of the court, together with costs, is not satisfied within the time specified in subrule (8), the clerk of court shall dispose of the property attached in execution in such a manner as shall be deemed most expedient in the interest of all the parties concerned, and shall apply the proceeds so obtained to the satisfaction of the judgment and all costs connected therewith, and shall pay the balance, if any, to the person whose goods have been attached in execution.

(16) Unless otherwise ordered by the court, the costs and expenses of issuing a warrant of execution and levying execution shall be a first charge on the proceeds of the property sold in execution, and may, so far as such proceeds are insufficient, be

recovered from the execution debtor as costs awarded by the court.

(17) No judgment creditor who obtains a warrant of execution from the court shall be entitled to share in or receive any part of the proceeds levied under any warrant of execution previously obtained, unless the judgment creditor has obtained such warrant within ten days from the day on which the previous warrant was obtained.

(18) Subject to the provisions of subrule (17) and to any hypothec existing prior to attachment, all warrants of execution lodged with the clerk of court on or before the day immediately preceding the date of the sale in execution shall rank *pro rata* in the distribution of the proceeds of the goods sold in execution.

(19) The clerk of the court shall attach to the warrant a statement of the result of the execution, showing the disposal of the amount recovered therefrom, attaching in support the receipts of the judgment creditor and showing the disposal of the balance, if any.

Additional provisions relating to the attachment of immovable property

24. (1) If the judgment debt has not been satisfied by the attachment of movable property, the process for the execution of judgment against immovable property shall be in terms of rule 23 subject to the provisions of this rule.

(2) A warrant of execution against immovable property shall state the situation and nature of the immovable property which is sought to be attached with sufficient detail so as to enable it to be identified precisely.

(3) The clerk of court may, by notice served in like manner as a summons, require the execution debtor to deliver up to him forthwith all documents in his possession or under his control relating in any way to the title to the property which is the subject of a warrant of execution.

(4) The clerk of court shall ascertain and record whether the property which is the subject of a warrant of execution is subject to any claim ranking in priority to that of the execution creditor.

(5) Any person who alleges a claim ranking in priority to that of the execution creditor may apply to the court to set aside the execution at any time before registration of transfer to the purchaser, and the court may, thereafter, make such order as it thinks just.

(6) The mode of attachment of immovable property shall be in the form of a notice given under the hand of the clerk of court and served, together with the warrant of execution, upon the Registrar of Deeds or his deputy, upon all holders of bonds which are registered against the attached property and, if the attached property is occupied by a person other than the execution debtor, upon such person.

(7) The clerk of court shall appoint a day and place for the sale of the attached property, such day being, except by special leave of the court, not less than one month after the service of the notice of attachment, and he shall cause the sale to be advertised at least twice in the *Gazette* and in some newspaper circulating in the district, which advertisement shall contain a short description of such property and its situation, the time and place of the sale and the material conditions thereof.

(8) The execution creditor shall appoint a conveyancer for the purposes of sale and transfer.

(9) The conditions of sale shall be prepared and delivered by the execution creditor to the clerk of court, with a copy to the execution debtor:

Provided that the execution debtor may bring the conditions of sale before the district commissioner for settlement on application made not more than four days after delivery of such conditions to the execution debtor.

(10) Subject to the provisions of subrule (11), the execution creditor or any person having an interest in the due and proper realization of such property may, by notice given to the clerk of court within fourteen days of the attachment, require that such property be sold by an auctioneer in the ordinary course of business and may in such notice nominate the auctioneer who is to be employed.

(11) Where a notice in terms of subrule (10) is given by any person other than the execution creditor, such notice shall be accompanied by the deposit of a sum sufficient to cover the additional expense of a sale by an auctioneer in the ordinary course of business, and, in default of such deposit, such notice shall be of no force and effect:

Provided that such notice shall lapse if the services of an auctioneer are not obtainable.

(12) If, after satisfying the execution creditor, there are sufficient surplus proceeds from the sale of the attached property, the depositor shall be refunded his deposit.

(13) If, after satisfying the execution creditor, there are insufficient surplus proceeds from the sale of the attached property, the deposit shall, as far as may be necessary, be applied in payment of the auctioneer's fees and expenses.

(14) If two or more notices are made in terms of subrule (10) the first shall have preference over all other notices.

(15) The sale shall be by public auction and the property shall, subject to the conditions of sale, be sold to the highest bidder.

(16) The sale shall be held at such place as the district commissioner may determine, and shall be held in the presence of the clerk of court or such other person as the district commissioner may appoint.

(17) The clerk of the court or other person appointed by the district commissioner in terms of subrule (16) shall issue a certificate stating whether

or not the sale was duly and properly conducted, the identity of the execution debtor, the purchaser of the property and the amount of the purchase price, and such certificate shall be proof of the said matters stated therein.

(18) If a certificate in terms of subrule (17) states that the sale was duly and properly executed, the district commissioner shall, subject to the provisions of any other law, authorize transfer to the purchaser upon payment by the purchaser of the purchase money and compliance by him with the conditions of sale.

(19) If a certificate in terms of subrule (17) states that the sale was not duly and properly conducted, the district commissioner shall declare the sale to be of no force and effect, and the clerk of the court shall readvertise and sell the property in accordance with these rules.

(20) After transfer of the property to the purchaser has been effected, the clerk of the court shall pay the judgment creditor the amount of his claim and costs, and any balance resulting thereafter shall, subject to the provisions of these rules, be paid to the judgment debtor, or, if he cannot be located, to the court.

Garnishee orders

25. Any application for a garnishee order for enforcement of a judgment shall be made *ex parte* to a magistrate's court by lodging such application with the clerk of that court.

Order 5

APPEALS

Appeal Procedure

26. (1) Any person against whom any final judgment of the court has been given may appeal against such

judgment to the Court of Appeal, and, if he intends to appeal, shall, within thirty days of such judgment, note his appeal to the Court of Appeal in the form DCC 7, and shall -

(a) pay a fee of ten dollars for noting the appeal; and

(b) .... (repealed)

(c) submit a statement setting forth concisely and under distinct headings the grounds of objecting to the judgment appealed against and stating the exact nature of the relief sought.

(2) All appeals not prosecuted within a period of three months from the date of the noting thereof shall be deemed to have been abandoned.

(3) When an appeal has been noted the clerk of court shall inform the appellant of the steps necessary to be taken by him for prosecuting such appeal and the court may, in its discretion, allow or delay the execution of judgment.

(4) If the court allows or delays the execution of judgment in terms of subrule (3), it may, in its discretion, require that such property as may be deemed adequate be deposited as security for the satisfaction of the judgment of the court of appeal.

(5) When an appeal is noted the district commissioner shall inform the respondent of this fact by causing to be served on him a notice in the form DCC 8.

(6) .... (repealed)

Order 6

COSTS, FEES AND DEPARTURE FROM RULES

Costs

27. The court, in giving judgment or making any order, including an adjournment and amendment, may make such order as to costs as it thinks just.

Fees

28. The fees payable in terms of these rules shall be as prescribed in the Second Schedule.

Departure from Rules

29. (1) The court may at any time depart from any of these Rules at its own instance or at the request of any party if in its opinion such departure is conducive to the ends of justice.

(2) Whenever it is necessary that any person should be joined as a co-plaintiff or co-defendant, the court shall take such steps as may be necessary to bring about such joinder.

(3) In these rules any reference to a claim shall *mutatis mutandis* include a counterclaim, and in any case in which a claim and counterclaim are being heard together, the court shall take such steps as may be necessary to ensure the proper hearing of the case.

Order 7

REPEAL OF EXISTING RULES

Repeals

30. The rules set out in the Third Schedule are hereby repealed.

First Schedule *(Rule 2)*

Forms

DCC 1	Record book
DCC 2	Summons
DCC 3	Subpoena
DCC 4	Warrant of execution
DCC 5	Court record jacket
DCC 6	Notice of hearing
DCC 7	Notice of appeal by appellant
DCC 8	Notice of appeal to respondent

Form DCC 1

DISTRICT COMMISSIONER'S COURT

Civil Record Book, District of ....

No.	Parties	Claim	Date of compl-iant	Date of issuing summons	Dates of hear-ing	Postpone-ments or adjourn-ments	Parties appear-ing and nature of defence	Judgment of the court	Subsequent proceedings and remarks

Form DCC 2

Case No. ......of 19....

RHODESIA

SUMMONS

In the Civil Case in District Commissioner's Court

TO ....living or working at

....

....

TAKE NOTICE that you are required to attend this office on .... the .... at 8.00 a.m. to answer the under-mentioned complaint made against you by .... You are to bring with you any witness you require.

....

District Commissioner

SINDEBELE:

Nxa ungafikanga ngalolu suku olulotshiweyo, lanxa ungayitholanga imvumo yeCourt ukubana ungezi, icala lizaphiwa wena ngokungafiki kwakho ukuzazulandulela.

Nxa kukhona ongakuqondiya kufuneka uyebuza kuDistrict Commissioner oseduzane lalapho okhona ngaphambi kwalolo suku mhlana icala lakhona lizathoniswa.

CHISONA:

Kana usina kusvika nomusi warehwa, wuyezwe usina kubvumirwa neCourt kuti urege kuuya, mhosva inozopiwa iwe nokusavepo kwako kuzoinzwa.

Kana paine chisingasanonzwika, wakafanira kunovunza kuna District Commissioner ari padyo nekwauri ikoko zuva rokutongwa kwenhosva yacho risati rasvika.

ENGLISH:

If you do not appear on the date shown and have not obtained the Court's permission to be absent, judgment will be given against you in your default.

In case of doubt you should consult the nearest District Commissioner before the day on which the case is to be heard.

Office .... Date ....19..

Complaint:

....

....

To Employers - Please note that this Summons is of the SAME LEGAL FORCE AND EFFECT AS ONE ISSUED BY THE MAGISTRATE'S COURT.

CONSENT TO JUDGMENT

I, ... admit that I am liable to the Plaintiff as claimed in this summons (or in the amount of $ ....) and costs to date and I hereby consent to judgment accordingly.

Dated this .... day of ....19..

....
Defendant

1. Witness: ....
2. Witness: ....

ENDORSEMENT OF SERVICE

(To be completed by the Messenger after service)

I hereby certify that I have personally served a true copy of this summons on the Defendant herein named and that I have explained to him/her to the best of my ability, the exigencies thereof.

....
Messenger of the Court

Date of Service ....

I hereby certify that I have made diligent search for the person to whom this summons is addressed, but have failed to find him.

....
Messenger of the Court

Date ....

Form DCC 3

SUBPOENA

in the Court of the District Commissioner ....

....

vs.

....

TO

OF

TAKE NOTICE that you are required to attend at this Court as a witness at .... on .... at 8.00 a.m.
If you are not called at 8.00 a.m. you are to remain in attendance until you are called or told by the Court that you may go.
If you fail to appear you may be liable to a fine of $100,00 or committed to gaol for 6 months.

Fee paid ....
Receipt No. ....

....
District Commissioner

Date ....

BONA UKUBA uyafuneka ukuthi ubesemthethwandaba njengomfakazi e .... mhlaka .... ngo 8.00 ekuseni.
Nxa ungabizwana ngo 8.00 ekuseni kumele uhlale ulindele uze ubizwe loba uze utshelwe ngumthethwandaba ukuthi ungahamba. Ungahlala ungabonakali ungafayindiswa imali engamadola alikhulu ($100,00) loba isiwe entilongweni iziyisithupha (6 months).

Fee paid ....
Receipt No. ....

Date ....

....
District Commissioner

UNOZIVISWA kuti unodikanwa kuva paCourt (Dare) rino

somufakazi (mboo) pano pa .... nomusi wa ...... nenguva dze 8.00 a.m.

Kana usina kushevedzwa ne nguva dze 8.00 a.m. uno ramba uripo kudakara washevedzwa kana kuudzwa nedare kuti enda hako. Kana ukasavapo ungaripiswa faindi $100,00 kana kuendeswa ku jeri (torongo) kwe mwedzi mitanhatu.

Fee paid ....

Receipt No. ....

Date ....

....
District Commissioner

I have received this subpoena. I understand it.

Date ....

I certify that I have today served a copy of this subpoena on the person to whom it is addressed. I have informed the witness of the names of the parties to the case and the date and place at which the witness must appear.

Date ....
Messenger of the Court

I certify that I have made diligent search for the person to whom this subpoena is addressed, but have failed to find him.

Date ....
Messenger of the Court

Form DCC 4

W.O.E. No. .... of 19 ....

WARRANT OF EXECUTION AGAINST PROPERTY

IN the DISTRICT COMMISSIONER'S COURT for the DISTRICT of

....

held at ....

between .... Plaintiff

and .... Defendant

TO THE MESSENGER OF THE COURT ....

Whereas in this action the said
on the day of 19 , by the judgment
of the court delivered against the said
of
the several sums set out in the margin hereof, amounting
in all to the sum of $

Amounts to be levied
(with costs of execution)

	$	c
Judgment Debt		
Costs		
Costs of Issuing Warrant		
Cost of Appeal		
Total		

This therefore to authoriz
and require you that of th
property of the said
you cause to be levied and
raised the said sum
of $
together with your costs
of this execution and pay
to the said
the said sum of $.
And return as required by
law what you have done by
virtue hereof, for which
this shall be your warrant

Dated at this day of 19 .
By Order of the Court

....
Clerk of the District Commissioner's Court

....
Attorney for Execution Creditor

Note. - (1) If the judgment debtor pays the amounts specified in the margin hereof, with messenger's charges of $ within half an hour after the entry of the messenger, he will not be required to pay any further costs of execution.

(2) This execution may be paid out before sale subject to the payment of the messenger's fees and charges of execution.

(3) The only immovable property upon which this warrant may be executed is

I certify that I have this .... day of .... 19..
served a true copy of this warrant of execution upon
.... at ....
and have fully explained the exigencies thereof
to him/her.

....

Date ....

I have received a copy of this warrant, and I
understand that I may not dispose of the property
which has been placed under attachment.

Judgment Debtor ....

LIST OF PROPERTY PLACED UNDER ATTACHMENT

....
....
....
....

I certify that I have made diligent search for the person named in this Warrant, but have been unable to locate him/her and have served the Warrant upon ...., a responsible person occupying the premises.

....

Date ....

Form DCC 5

RHODESIA

CIVIL RECORD

IN THE COURT OF THE DISTRICT COMMISSIONER

FOR THE DISTRICT OF ....

HELD AT

Case No. ,..... of 19 ..

In the matter of

.... Plaintiff

versus

.... Defendant

Claim: Amount ....

Plea ....

Reply ....

Date ....

Clerk of the Court

Postponed to .... at ....

to .... at ....

to .... at ....

JUDGMENT ....

....

....

....

Date ....

District Commissioner

COSTS Fees: Claim Fee ....

Service Fee ....

Form DCC 6

IN THE COURT OF THE DISTRICT COMMISSIONER

....

NOTICE OF HEARING

Case No: ....

....
vs

....

Take notice that the hearing of the above case which was set down for .... has been postponed to .... at 8 a.m.

Bona ukuba ukuthethwa kwecala elingaphezulu okwankmiselwe mhlaka .... sekuntshintshelwe kumhlaka .... ngo 8.00 ekuseni.
Unoziviswa kuti kutongwa kwe mhosva yakanyorwa pamusoro iyi yaizotongwa nomusi wa .... yambo miswa kusvikira musi wa .... nenguva dze 8.00 a.m.

Date ....
Clerk of the Court

I certify that I have served a copy of the above notice on .... on ....

....

I acknowledge receipt of a copy of this notice.

Witness: ....

Date ....

Form DCC 7

IN THE COURT OF THE DISTRICT COMMISSIONER ....

NOTICE OF APPEAL BY APPELLANT

Case No. ....

....

....

Judgment by .... on ....

NOTICE OF APPEAL

I, ... Plaintiff/Defendant

in this case, hereby give notice of appeal

against the judgment

Date ....

Appellant

I *want/do NOT want* to be present at the hearing of the appeal

I *shall/shall NOT* be represented by a lawyer at the appeal

....

Appellant

$10,00 NOTING FEE attached to original cover of case.

....

Clerk of Court

Form DCC 8

IN THE COURT OF THE DISTRICT COMMISSIONER

Case No. ....

NOTICE OF APPEAL TO RESPONDENT

....
vs.

....

To ....

I hereby notify you that ....
has lodged an appeal against the judgment in this case.

....
Clerk of Court

I *want/do NOT want* to be present for the hearing of this appeal

I *shall/shall NOT* be represented by a lawyer at the appeal

My lawyer is ....

....
Respondent

Date ....

Witness ....

Second Schedule *(Rules 3, 6, 14, 23 and 28)*

FEES

Nature of document	*Relevant section of the rules*	*Amount*
Claim for all causes of	Rule 3 (2)	$5,00
Claim for divorce	Rule 3 (2)	$10,00
Subpoena	Rule 6 (2)	$0,25
Set of interrogat-ories	Rule 14 (1)	$2,00
Warrant of execution	Rule 23 (1)	$1,00 plus $0,10 on each dollar in excess of $200,00
Extract of judgment	Rule 28	$1,00
Copies of record	Rule 28	$0,30 per page with a minimum fee of $2,00
Taxing a bill of costs	Rule 28	$1,00

Third Schedule *(Rule 30)*

REPEALS

Rules	*Rhodesia Government Notice No.*
District Commissioners Courts (Civil Procedure) Rules 1928 ..	364 of 1928
Native Commissioners Courts (Civil Procedure) (Amendment) Rules, 1947 (No. 1) ..	225 of 1947

Rules		*Rhodesia Government Notice No.*
Native Commissioners Courts (Civil Procedure) (Amendment) Rules, 1951 (No. 2)	..	932 of 1951
Native Commissioners Courts (Civil Procedure) (Amendment) Rules, 1961 (No. 3)	..	457 of 1961
District Commissioners Courts (Civil Procedure) (Amendment) Rules, 1963 (No. 4)	..	320 of 1963

APPENDIX II

RULES OF THE COURT OF APPEAL FOR AFRICAN CIVIL CASES

R.G.N. 116/1960; 300/1960

---

1. These rules may be cited as the Court of Appeal for Native Civil Cases Rules, 1960.

Definitions

2. In these rules unless inconsistent with the context -

'Act' means the African Affairs Act *(Chapter 228)*, as amended;

'court' means the Court of Appeal for African civil cases established under section 6 of the Act;

'appeal' shall include cross appeal;

'appellant' means any person entitled to appeal to the court in terms of the Act;

'lower court' means the court of a district commissioner or district officer against whose judgment the appeal is lodged;

'clerk' means the clerk of the lower court.

'President' means the President of the Court;

'record' means the aggregate of papers relating to an appeal (including the pleadings, proceedings, evidence and judgments) which are laid before the court on the hearing of an appeal;

'registrar' means the registrar of the court and includes an assistant registrar.

'respondent' means any person who has been served with notice of appeal or who is entitled to be so served;

'legal representative' includes an advocate or an attorney of the High Court or an articled clerk entitled to appear in the lower court;

'messenger' means the messenger of the lower court and shall include his deputy;

'service' means personal service through the messenger of the lower court or through such other person as is duly delegated to effect personal service by the lower court or such other form of substituted service as is authorized by the appeal court.

Appeals

3. Sessions of the court shall be held and the time venue and forum for all such sessions and for the hearing of appeals shall be settled in accordance with directions given by the President.

4. (1) (a) Every appeal shall be instituted in the form of a notice of appeal signed by the appellant or his legal representative and shall be noted within 30 days of the date of the giving of judgment.

(b) The appellant shall deliver or cause to be delivered such notice to the clerk who shall note its contents and forward it to the registrar together with the original record and three copies thereof certified by the clerk and at the same time the appellant shall serve a certified copy of such notice on the respondent.

(c) On receipt of any notice of appeal the registrar shall date and file such notice.

(2) Any notice of appeal shall set forth concisely and under distinct heads the grounds of objection to the judgment appealed against stating the exact nature of the relief which is sought.

5. (1) The notice of appeal shall be served on the respondent within 30 days of the date of the noting of the appeal.

(2) The registrar shall not accept any notice of appeal which is presented after the expiration of the period specified in subrule (1) of this rule unless leave to appeal out of time has been obtained previously in accordance with the provisions of rule 6.

(3) Any application for an extension of time within which to file a notice of appeal may be filed with the registrar.

6. (1) Any application for an extension of time within which to note an appeal shall be made to the court through the registrar stating shortly the reasons upon which the application is based. Where facts are alleged, the application shall be supported and verified by affidavit. At the time any such application is made a copy of the application and supporting affidavit shall be served on the respondent by the applicant.

(2) Any respondent shall have the right to file a reply and supporting affidavits within seven days of service on him of the application.

(3) (a) Any such application shall be set down for hearing by the registrar of the court, in accordance with such directions as may be given by the President.

(b) The court may hear evidence to determine the merits of the application but only after giving notice to all parties concerned.

(c) After evidence has been heard to determine the application it shall be competent for the court to proceed with the appeal forthwith if the parties are agreeable.

(3) (d) The application may be granted or refused subject to such order as to costs as the court deems fit.

7. Either the applicant or the respondent may intimate to the registrar directly or through the clerk who shall transmit the information to the registrar that he does not seek to be present in person or legally represented at the hearing of an appeal.

8. (1) An appellant may at any time before the hearing abandon his appeal by giving notice of abandonment in writing to the registrar and on such notice being given the appeal shall be deemed to have been dismissed by the court subject to such orders as to costs as the court deems fit.

(2) The registrar shall give notice of such dismissal and any order as to costs thereon to the respondent and the clerk of the lower court.

9. (1) The registrar shall on the instructions of the President cause notice of the date and place of hearing to be served upon the appellant and respondent.

(2) The court may hear and determine an appeal without giving notice to any person who has intimated in terms of rule 7 that he does not wish to attend the hearing.

10. If for any reason it appears proper to the court to adjourn an appeal or application the court may do so on such terms and for such period as it may in its discretion determine.

11. The court shall have the power to direct that in any case on appeal the proceedings be re-opened for the taking of any evidence or in relation to any other matter and any additional evidence or other matter so directed by the court may be taken or dealt with either before the court itself or before the lower court or before any native commissioner or assistant native commissioner.

12. Any costs awarded by the court may be taxed by the registrar. Such taxation may be taken on review by either party before the President.

13. The registrar shall file with the record of each appeal a copy of the judgement of the court signed by the President together with a copy of the order signed by the registrar. The registrar shall then furnish a duplicate signed copy of the judgement and the order thereon to each of the parties to the appeal.

14. Notice of appeal from the decision of the court shall be lodged with the registrar within 21 days from the date of such decision.

15. To facilitate the just decision of any matter the President may extend any time laid down by these rules subject to such order as to costs as the President may think fit.

GLOSSARY OF CUSTOMARY LAW TERMS

NB. *Where native terms are recognized as of common usage a translation is unnecessary. The best guide is words that have already been accepted in their meaning in recognized customs or decided cases or in both need not be translated to offer guidance to the court as to their meaning* - Misheki *v* Eniya 1960 SRN 685.

Chipanda	a system based on the principle that cattle received in connection with the marriage of a daughter should be used in payment of *lobolo* to provide a wife for her brother - *Gariwa* v *Chigwedere Musharurgwa* 1958 SRN 533.
Chiredzwa	rearing fee for an illegitimate child, payable by the father to the mother's family - *Mucheneripi* v *Komponi* 1951 SRN 286. Payment is made only if the father of the child does not have custody thereof - *Mado* v *Skudamedzi* 1942 SRN 193.
Chisaba or Chishawa	a beast, formerly a goat, paid by the seducer of a virgin or her first husband for the act of deflowering, dedicated to the ancestral spirit of the girl's family- *Mashako Pombi* v *Stephen Chimombe* 1953 SRN 412.
Dombo	emissary or go-between in marriage negotiations - a *munyai* - *Madziwa* v *Chirenda* 1939 SRN 63.
Isondhlo	(Sindebele), a payment to one person by another for the maintenance of a third. A universal term among the Nguni-speaking people of Southern Africa (Shona equivalent is *Urere*) - *Ginza* v *Johannes* 1936 SRN 92.

	It is not payable by a father of children whose marriage breaks down after full *lobolo* has been paid - *Sitayi* v *Lomacala and Mhlanga* 1931 SRN 33; *Mkamange* v *Tamange* 1949 SRN 207.
Kucheka Ukama	a public ceremony before the chief performed by a couple who are unable to marry each other because their consanguineous relationship is prohibitive of marriage, carried out formally to sever that relationship - *Mtanda* v *Shiota* 1929 SRN 5.
Kuronza	the obligation of a herdsman strictly to account for all increase and deaths in the cattle he herds on behalf of another - *Manuka* v *Makanyesi* 1942 SRN 162.
Lobolo	'marriage consideration' or 'bride wealth'. A marriage settlement paid by the husband to his wife's parents or guardian, for the benefit of the woman and her offspring, and symbolizing the transfer of the woman from her own family to that of the husband - *R* v *Gutayi & others* 1915 SR 49.
Masungira	see *Chisbaba*
Mereka	damages for seduction - *Anderson* v *Mariya* 1929 SRN 23.
Mombe yo amai	the beast handed over by the suitor to the bride's mother. It is an essential element of a customary marriage - *Tambi* v *Sailos* 1953 SRN 356.
Munyai	emissary in marriage negotiations - a *dombo* - *Robert* v *Mugwagwa* 1954 SRN 458.

Muripo	a payment in the nature of a fine for seduction paid to the father of the girl, to atone for the wrong done - *Kapisi* v *Magwayi* 1937 SRN 10.
Rubvunso	originally the passing of a hoe, now a payment of money forming part of the *rutsambo* which is brought by the *munyai* to the prospective wife's family. When the father of the girl accepts the *rubvinzo* payment it constitutes the formal acceptance of the suitability of the suitor and consent to the marriage. The payment is returnable only if the girl herself then rejects the suitor before marriage - - *Mafinde* v *Mashamu* 1949 SRN 192.
Rutsambo or Kangaziwe	a payment made in contemplation of marriage which may in certain circumstances be returnable on dissolution of the marriage - *Jambawumadondo* v *Mudzamiri* 1973 AAC 24.
Shashiko	a woman's front apron. Formerly for a woman spontaneously to tear off her *shashiko* and strike her paramour with it raised a presumption of guilt in the man, in an action for adultery - *Makonzenkenyi* v *Paradzanyi* 1928 SRN 42; now becoming archaic.
Uhlenga	(Ndebele) payment for the manumission of a slave - obsolete - *Mabigwa* v *Matibini* 1946 SRN 117.
Ukubuyisa	(Ndebele) ceremony of the distribution of a deceased estate - *Magwisi* v *Kombayi* 1947 SRN 177.

Urere (Chishona) maintenance paid for children of a marriage when custody is awarded to the father but because of age the children are being cared for by the mother - *Ginza* v *Johannes* 1936 SRN 92.

Ushamavanga a token payment by way of atonement when one person unintentionally causes bodily injury to another - *George* v *Gabaza* 1948 SRN 187.

I N D E X

NB. *The subject-matter of the rules of court, contained between pages 85 and 132 are not indexed: where relevant, the individual heading to each rule adequately conveys the content thereof.*

ADMINISTRATION OF ESTATES ACT *(CHAPTER 301)*
    s. 69, 7, 80
ADULTERY
    burden of proof, 38
    Christian marriage, defence to, 51
    collusion, effect of, 57
    condonation, effect of, 56
    damages, grounds for, 56
    degree of proof, 56
    evidence in, 38
    marriage unregistered, no cause of action for, 57
    plaintiff, onus on to prove, 57
    presumption that took place, 56
    that woman unmarried, allegation no defence, 57
AFRICAN
    defined, 1, 8
    foreign, custody of children, 67
    foreign, effect on marriage, 53
AFRICAN AFFAIRS ACT *(CHAPTER 228)*
    s. 2, 2
    s. 4 (4), 5
    s.5, 7,8
    s.5 (3), 26
    s.5 (7), 34
    s.6 (1), (2), 5
    s.6 (3), (6), 6
    s.6 (8), 5
AFRICAN LAW AND TRIBAL COURTS ACT *(CHAPTER 237)*
    Part II, 9-10, 19
    s.2, 1
    s.3 (1), (2), 3
    s.3 (3), 4, 54
    s.4, 4

AFRICAN LAW, etc *(cont)*
    s.5, 2
    s.24, 5
AFRICAN MARRIAGES ACT *(CHAPTER 238)*
    policy of, 42
    s. 3 (3), 66
    s. 7 (1), 52
    s. 11 (1), 48
AFRICAN WILLS ACT *(CHAPTER 240)*, 82
APPEAL
    abandoning, 32
    adjournment of, 33
    Appellate Division, to 34
    fee, 32
    new point taken on, 29
    notice, 29
    " contents of, 29
    noting of, 28
    out of time, 30
    " " " condonation, factors affecting, 31
    procedure on, 28
    time of, 28
ASSOCIATIONS, citing of, 9
CATTLE
    damages not to be assessed in terms of, 25
    herdsmen, actions against, 79
    liability for trespass of, 78
    ownership of, by a woman, 59
    " transfer of, *lobolo* payments, 46, 79
CHIEF
    arbitrator, as, 10-11
    as assessor, in District Commissioner's Court, 8
    court, relevance of proceedings before, 19
    defined, 2
    jurisdiction in tribal court, 9
CHILDREN
    acts of, liability for, 76
    conceived during marriage, presumption of paternity, 40
    custody, award of, to encourage payment of *lobolo*, 44
    custody, award of, normally to father, 64, 65
    " " " to mother, 63,67

CHILDREN *(cont)*
custody, award of to mother, maintenance of, 68
" " " to other than parent, 66
" " " adulterine, 64, 67
" " " court not bound by agreement of parents, 67
custody, award of, father debarred from, 67
" " " " forfeiting rights, 67
" " " foreigners, law applicable, 67
" " " issue between parents, 66
" " " child of tender years, 65
" " " removal to father, 66
" " " when issue not canvassed, 54
" " " claims for, 71
" " " woman to be assisted by her guardian, 67
" " " in event of father's death, 64
effect of payment of *lobolo*, 45
guardianship of, 64-65
heir, rights in respect of, 82
illegitimate, custody and guardianship, 70-71
incestuous, father no claim to, 71
legitimacy of, 40, 72
moral and material welfare paramount, 31,63,64,65, 66,70,71
particulars of, to be recorded, 16
rearing fee, 69
CHIPANDA
nature of, 49
no right to more than one, 49
CHISABA
nature of, 49
no recovery of on dissolution of marriage, 49
CLERK OF COURT
appeal, notice to, 29
duty on receipt of claim, 13
setting down cases, 13
COSTS
assessment of, approach, 26
award, discretion to make, 34
disapproval of action, by court, 27
expenses, inclusion of, appeal, 34
plaintiff, may not be penalized, 27

COURT OF APPEAL
appeals, approach to, 29
appeal from, 5
assessors, who are eligible, 5
assistance to, by furnishing reasons for judgment, 26
costs, orders for, by, 6
damages, interference with, by, 33
decisions of, 6
evidence in, 40
judgment, interference with, by, 33
powers of, 6
president, appointment of, 5
remittal by, 33
review jurisdiction, none, 40
sittings, 6, 29
CUSTOMARY LAW
application, 3
ascertainment, 2
changes in, seduction, 61
defined, 1
foreign, effect on marriage, 53
policy as regards, 4
presumption of, 4
repugnant to natural justice or morality, 4
DAMAGES
adultery, 57
assessment of, 23
assault, basis of assessment, 75
award, interference by court of appeal, 33
before *lobolo*, in actions for seduction, 60
defamation, assessment, 77
difficulty, duty of court, 23
seduction, assessment, factors affecting, 60
" postponement of award until child born, 61
" of prostitute, 62
" measure of, 59
DEFAMATION
action, limitations on, 76
damages for, assessment, 77
defence to, 77
privileged occasions, 77
DEFAULT JUDGMENT
not a final judgment, 28
notice of, 28

DEFENDANT
adultery, defence to, 57
" in actions for, evidence in denial, 38
" collusion, onus on to prove, 57
court not to advise, 19
default, in, procedure on, 23
estopped from appealing against own plea, 28
" " " " consent to judgment, 28
judgment, consent to, 14
plea, accuracy of, determination, 18
" admission or denial, 18
res judicata, plea of, 19
summons, service on, 14
DEFINITIONS
African, 1, 8
chief, 2
Customary law, 1
Enactment, 2
heir at African law, 82
natural heir, 80
tribe, 2
DELICT
accidental injury, 74
animal, liability of owner, 75
assault, competence of action, 75
" nature of claim, 75
children, liability for acts of, 76
malice, proof of essential, 74
malicious proceedings, 77-78
negligence, 78
DISTRICT COMMISSIONER
administrative decisions, 8
assessor, as, in court of appeal, 5
costs, approach to assessment of, 26
court, holding of, 6
disputes in terms of the African Wills Act, 82
jurisdiction in disputes between chief and kraal-head, 8
jurisdiction when ousted, 7
DISTRICT COMMISSIONER'S COURT
addresses to, 22
chief as assessor in, 8

DISTRICT COMMISSIONER'S COURT *(cont)*
- claim, reading of, 17
  - " receiving of, 13
- custody of children, court may call witnesses, 65
- evidence in, 35 *et seq.*
- formality, minimum amount, 17
- holding of, 6
- judgment by, 24
- jurisdiction, 7
  - " no equitable to dissolve marriage, 54
  - " none to divorce action in unregistered marriage, 54
- maintenance, discretion to award, 58
- object of, 12
- proceedings in, record of, 16
- witness within precincts, calling of, 21

DIVORCE
- conjugal rights, not to each other, 51
- Christian marriage, law applicable, 50
  - " " wife, assistance by her guardian, 51
  - " " adultery, defendant in default, procedure, 51
  - " " restitution of conjugal rights, 5[illegible]
  - " " specific grounds, 51
- customary marriage, general, 54
  - " " adultery and desertion as grounds for, 55
  - " " impotence of husband as ground, 55
  - " " incompatibility not a ground, 55
  - " " malicious desertion, 55
  - " " physical cruelty, 55
  - " " specific grounds, 54
- evidence of valid marriage, 38
- foreigner, effect on marriage, 53

EVIDENCE
- adultery, in, 38
  - " proof of, 56
- assault, in assessment of damages, 75
- confession, 35
  - " duty of court, 36
  - " in seduction, importance of, 36

EVIDENCE *(cont)*
consent by, undesirable, 35
corroboration, what is meant by, 36
court of appeal, in, 40
criminal records, as, 35
lobolo, evidence of payment, 39
marriage, of valid, 38
medical report, adducing, 35
munyai, of, 37
non-expert, inadmissible, 36
paternity, of, 72
presumptions (see PRESUMPTIONS)
previous case, as, 35
proof, degree of generally, 35
scanty, procedure, 22
seduction, in cases of, 37
sufficiency of, 36
witness within precincts of court, calling of, 21
GUARDIAN
woman as, 59
woman, assisting, 16
GUARDIANSHIP
child of, normally to father, 64, 68
" " determination on death of father, 65
" " not awarded to person himself subject to, 68
HIGH COURT
Appellate Division, appeal to, 5
" " " from decision of magistrate, 7
General Division, no jurisdiction generally, 5
" " review jurisdiction, 40-41
notice of appeal, time for, 34
INTERPRETATION ACT *(CHAPTER 1)*
s. 3, 2
s. 34, 14
JUDGMENT
cattle in, incompetent, 25
default (see DEFAULT JUDGMENT)
errors in, correction of, 25
interference with, by court of appeal, 33
particulars of, sufficiency, 24
procedure on, 24
reasons for, 26

JUDICIAL OFFICER
evidence, clarification by, 22
matters before one, to be taken *de novo* before another, 20
recusal of, 21
LOBOLO
agreement on, essential, 44
" " exception to, 44
assessment of amount, 43
claim for return in unregistered marriage, 54
evidence of amount paid, 39
failure to pay, discouragement of, method, 44
heir, responsibility of, 81
nature of, 42
pledging - illegal, 48
recovery before marriage, 45
return of, date of valuation of amount paid, 46
" " factors affecting, 46-47
" " factors governing, 45
" " on proportionate basis, 46
rights arising from payment, 45
specific performance, not to be ordered, 44
subsidiary payments, 49
uncle, position of if providing, 45
MAGISTRATE'S COURT
Act, 7
jurisdiction in intestate succession, 80
s. 13 (1) (b) of Act, 7
MAINTENANCE
by woman's father, no claim on husband, 58, 69
children of, amount and duration of payment of, 68
" " custody awarded to mother, 68
court, discretion of, 58
illegitimate child, father not legally liable for, 70
law applicable, 69
lying-in expenses, as, 72
rearing fee, 69
seduction, pregnancy resulting, effect, 62
widow, of, 62-63
MAINTENANCE ACT *(CHAPTER 35)*
s. 6 (2) 70
s. 10, 58

MARRIAGE
unregistered, claim for return of *lobolo*, 54
Christian, common law applicable, 50
" governed by fixed principles, 64
" legal consequences of, 50
customary, essentials of, 52
domicile, effect of, on, 53
donations between spouses, 54
lobolo, role of in, 43
" return on dissolution, 46
officer, duty of, 52
promise to marry, breach of, no cause of action, 53, 61
MATRIMONIAL CAUSES ACT *(CHAPTER 39)*
s. 2 (3), (4), 52
s. 9, 58
MESSENGER OF COURT
summons, service by, 14
vernacular designation, 14
MUNYAI
evidence of in seduction cases, 37
role of in marriage negotiations, 43
NGOMBE YO AMAI
essential incident of marriage, 49
no entitlement if marriage negotiations break down, 62
not recoverable on dissolution of marriage, 49
PARTIES
addresses by, 22
advice to, by judicial officer, 21
appeal, advice of right to, 30
costs, 27
court, advice to, by, 20
cross-examination, 21
default, in, 23
domicilium citandi, obtaining of at trial, 32
expenses in costs of appeal, 34
representation desirable, 27
representation of, 15
PERSONAL RIGHTS
carriers, liability of, 83
deposit, decided by common law, 84
illegal contracts generally, 84
illegal contract of carriage, 83
payment of debt, proof, 84

PLAINTIFF
adducing evidence, 19
adultery cases, onus of, 57
damages, estimate of, acceptance, 24
default, procedure on, 23
loss, duty to mitigate, 23
penalizing for exercising rights, incompetent, 27
PLEDGING
illegal as regards *lobolo* payments, 48
PRESUMPTIONS
adultery of, 56
cohabitation, of, 39
legitimacy, of, 40
paternity after marriage, 40
" on seduction, 72
shashiko, none in relation to, 39
virginity, of, 39
woman, as to paternity, 39
" incompetent to enter contract, 58
PROCEEDINGS
claim, reading of, 17
conduct of, 19
language conducted in, 17
remittal, procedure, 34
to be recorded, 16
PROCESS
service, effective, 15
PROPERTY
immovable, no cause of action in customary law, 79
inheriting by a widow, 62, 79
REGISTRAR
appeal, notice of abandonment to, 32
notice of set-down, service of, 32
RUBVUNSO
seduction acceptance of, no claim, 62
when returnable, 49
RUTSAMBO
nature of, 48
not returnable after consummation of marriage, 48
separation from *lobolo*, 43
SEDUCTION
action for, when lies, 59
claim to children on, no, 70

SEDUCTION *(cont)*
damages for, assessment, factors to consider, 60
" " measure of, 59
" " before *lobolo*, 60
" " conditions, 60
" " nature of, 60
pregnancy resulting, procedure on confirmation, 61
" " loss of earnings, effect, 62
prostitute, of, 62
rubvunzo accepted, no claim, 70
virgins, Ndebele custom, 61
SUCCESSION
heir entitled to custody and guardianship of children, 82
'heir at African law' defined, 82
intestate, natural heir, general rule, 80
" " " exceptions, 81
" " " disinheritance, 81
" statutory provisions, 82
kurova guwa ceremony, 82
position of women, 81
testate, position of common law, 83
" disposition of property, 82
" disputes referred to district commissioner, 82
" statutory provisions, 82
SUMMONS
adultery, delay in issue of, effect, 57
particulars of, 13
service of, 14
TRIAL
domicilium citandi, obtaining at conclusion of, 32
postponement, 18
TRIBE
defined, 2
foreign, effect on marriage, 53
not a corporate entity, 8
WITNESS
assessment of, in judgment, 25, 26
attendance of, securing, 14
court not to call, 20
cross-examination of, 21
custody matters, may be called by court, 65

WITNESS *(cont)*
failure to attend, postponement on, 18
hostile, 21
interrogatories, examination by, 22
questioning by court, 21, 22
swearing of, 18
WOMEN
adultery, effect on value of, 56
consent of to marriage, essential, 52
guardian, as 59
" assistance by, 16, 67
husband entitled to wages of, 59
inheritance of property by, 62, 81
locus standi in judicio, 15
owning of property by, 59
presumptions re (see PRESUMPTIONS)
reconciliation attempt, effect of, 55
seduction, cannot sue for own, 59
trustee, as, 81
widow, inheritance of, 63
" maintenance of, 62-63